Characterizing and Communicating Uncertainty in the Assessment of Benefits and Risks of Pharmaceutical Products

Workshop Summary

I0896238

Denise Caruso, Rebecca A. English, and Anne B. Claiborne, *Rapporteurs*

Forum on Drug Discovery, Development, and Translation

Board on Health Sciences Policy

INSTITUTE OF MEDICINE
OF THE NATIONAL ACADEMIES

THE NATIONAL ACADEMIES PRESS
Washington, D.C.
www.nap.edu

THE NATIONAL ACADEMIES PRESS 500 Fifth Street, NW Washington, DC 20001

NOTICE: The workshop that is the subject of this workshop summary was approved by the Governing Board of the National Research Council, whose members are drawn from the councils of the National Academy of Sciences, the National Academy of Engineering, and the Institute of Medicine.

This activity was supported by contracts between the National Academy of Sciences and the U.S. Department of Health and Human Services (HHSN26300023 [Under Base #HHSN263201200074I] and HHSF22301026T [Under Base #HHSF223200810020I]), AbbVie Inc., American Diabetes Association, American Society for Microbiology, Amgen Inc., Association of American Medical Colleges, AstraZeneca, Burroughs Wellcome Fund, Critical Path Institute, Doris Duke Charitable Foundation, Eli Lilly and Company, *FasterCures*, Friends of Cancer Research, GlaxoSmithKline, Johnson & Johnson, March of Dimes Foundation, Merck & Co., Inc., Novartis Pharmaceuticals Corporation, Pfizer Inc., and Sanofi. The views presented in this publication do not necessarily reflect the views of the organizations or agencies that provided support for the activity.

International Standard Book Number-13: 978-0-309-31000-0
International Standard Book Number-10: 0-309-31000-8

Additional copies of this workshop summary are available for sale from the National Academies Press, 500 Fifth Street, NW, Keck 360, Washington, DC 20001; (800) 624-6242 or (202) 334-3313; http://www.nap.edu.

For more information about the Institute of Medicine, visit the IOM home page at: **www.iom.edu.**

Printed in the United States of America

The serpent has been a symbol of long life, healing, and knowledge among almost all cultures and religions since the beginning of recorded history. The serpent adopted as a logotype by the Institute of Medicine is a relief carving from ancient Greece, now held by the Staatliche Museen in Berlin.

Suggested citation: IOM (Institute of Medicine). 2014. *Characterizing and communicating uncertainty in the assessment of benefits and risks of pharmaceutical products: Workshop summary.* Washington, DC: The National Academies Press.

"Knowing is not enough; we must apply.
Willing is not enough; we must do."

—Goethe

INSTITUTE OF MEDICINE

OF THE NATIONAL ACADEMIES

Advising the Nation. Improving Health.

THE NATIONAL ACADEMIES

Advisers to the Nation on Science, Engineering, and Medicine

The **National Academy of Sciences** is a private, nonprofit, self-perpetuating society of distinguished scholars engaged in scientific and engineering research, dedicated to the furtherance of science and technology and to their use for the general welfare. Upon the authority of the charter granted to it by the Congress in 1863, the Academy has a mandate that requires it to advise the federal government on scientific and technical matters. Dr. Ralph J. Cicerone is president of the National Academy of Sciences.

The **National Academy of Engineering** was established in 1964, under the charter of the National Academy of Sciences, as a parallel organization of outstanding engineers. It is autonomous in its administration and in the selection of its members, sharing with the National Academy of Sciences the responsibility for advising the federal government. The National Academy of Engineering also sponsors engineering programs aimed at meeting national needs, encourages education and research, and recognizes the superior achievements of engineers. Dr. C. D. Mote, Jr., is president of the National Academy of Engineering.

The **Institute of Medicine** was established in 1970 by the National Academy of Sciences to secure the services of eminent members of appropriate professions in the examination of policy matters pertaining to the health of the public. The Institute acts under the responsibility given to the National Academy of Sciences by its congressional charter to be an adviser to the federal government and, upon its own initiative, to identify issues of medical care, research, and education. Dr. Victor J. Dzau is president of the Institute of Medicine.

The **National Research Council** was organized by the National Academy of Sciences in 1916 to associate the broad community of science and technology with the Academy's purposes of furthering knowledge and advising the federal government. Functioning in accordance with general policies determined by the Academy, the Council has become the principal operating agency of both the National Academy of Sciences and the National Academy of Engineering in providing services to the government, the public, and the scientific and engineering communities. The Council is administered jointly by both Academies and the Institute of Medicine. Dr. Ralph J. Cicerone and Dr. C. D. Mote, Jr., are chair and vice chair, respectively, of the National Research Council.

www.national-academies.org

PLANNING COMMITTEE ON CHARACTERIZING AND COMMUNICATING UNCERTAINTY IN THE ASSESSMENT OF BENEFITS AND RISKS OF PHARMACEUTICAL PRODUCTS[1]

BARUCH FISCHHOFF (*Co-Chair*), Carnegie Mellon University, Pittsburgh, PA
ROBERT E. RATNER (*Co-Chair*), American Diabetes Association, Alexandria, VA
MARGARET ANDERSON, *FasterCures*, Washington, DC
CHRISTOPHER P. AUSTIN, National Center for Advancing Translational Sciences, Bethesda, MD
PATRICK J. FREY, Center for Drug Evaluation and Research, Silver Spring, MD
TAREK A. HAMMAD, Merck & Co., Inc., North Wales, PA
GAVIN HUNTLEY-FENNER, Huntley-Fenner Advisors, Irvine, CA
CHARLES F. MANSKI, Northwestern University, Evanston, IL
PAUL J. SELIGMAN, Amgen Inc., Washington, DC
LANA R. SKIRBOLL, Sanofi, Washington, DC
BRIAN L. STROM, Rutgers, the State University of New Jersey, Newark
MYRL WEINBERG, National Health Council, Washington, DC
STEVEN WOLOSHIN, Dartmouth Medical School, Hanover, NH

IOM Staff

ANNE B. CLAIBORNE, Forum Director
REBECCA A. ENGLISH, Program Officer
ELIZABETH F. C. TYSON, Associate Program Officer
BARRET ZIMMERMANN, Senior Program Assistant (until July 2014)
ANDREW M. POPE, Director, Board on Health Sciences Policy

[1] Institute of Medicine planning committees are solely responsible for organizing the workshop, identifying topics, and choosing speakers. The responsibility for the published workshop summary rests with the workshop rapporteurs and the institution.

FORUM ON DRUG DISCOVERY, DEVELOPMENT, AND TRANSLATION[1]

JEFFREY M. DRAZEN (*Co-Chair*), *New England Journal of Medicine*, Boston, MA
STEVEN K. GALSON (*Co-Chair*), Amgen Inc., Thousand Oaks, CA
RUSS BIAGIO ALTMAN, Stanford University, CA
MARGARET ANDERSON, *FasterCures*, Washington, DC
HUGH AUCHINCLOSS, National Institute of Allergy and Infectious Diseases, Bethesda, MD
CHRISTOPHER P. AUSTIN, National Center for Advancing Translational Sciences, Bethesda, MD
ANN C. BONHAM, Association of American Medical Colleges, Washington, DC
LINDA BRADY, National Institute of Mental Health, Bethesda, MD
GAIL H. CASSELL, Harvard Medical School (Visiting), Carmel, IN
ANDREW M. DAHLEM, Eli Lilly and Company, Indianapolis, IN
JAMES H. DOROSHOW, National Cancer Institute, Bethesda, MD
GARY L. FILERMAN, Atlas Health Foundation, McLean, VA
MARK J. GOLDBERGER, AbbVie Inc., Rockville, MD
HARRY B. GREENBERG, Stanford University School of Medicine, CA
KATHY L. HUDSON, National Institutes of Health, Bethesda, MD
LYNN D. HUDSON, Critical Path Institute, Tucson, AZ
S. CLAIBORNE JOHNSTON, Dell Medical School, University of Texas, Austin
MICHAEL KATZ, March of Dimes Foundation, White Plains, NY
JACK D. KEENE, Duke University Medical Center, Durham, NC
RUSTY KELLEY, Burroughs Wellcome Fund, Research Triangle Park, NC
RONALD L. KRALL, University of Pittsburgh, Steamboat Springs, CO
FREDA C. LEWIS-HALL, Pfizer Inc., New York, NY
CAROL MIMURA, University of California, Berkeley
BRIGGS W. MORRISON, AstraZeneca, Summit, NJ
BERNARD H. MUNOS, InnoThink Center for Research in Biomedical Innovation, Indianapolis, IN
ELIZABETH (BETSY) MYERS, Doris Duke Charitable Foundation, New York, NY
JOHN J. ORLOFF, Baxter BioScience, Deerfield, IL
RAJESH RANGANATHAN, National Institute of Neurological Disorders and Stroke, Bethesda, MD

---

[1] Institute of Medicine forums and roundtables do not issue, review, or approve individual documents. The responsibility for the published workshop summary rests with the workshop rapporteurs and the institution.

ROBERT E. RATNER, American Diabetes Association, Alexandria, VA
MICHAEL ROSENBLATT, Merck & Co., Inc., Whitehouse Station, NJ
JAMES S. SHANNON, GlaxoSmithKline, Brentford, Middlesex, UK
ELLEN V. SIGAL, Friends of Cancer Research, Washington, DC
LANA R. SKIRBOLL, Sanofi, Washington, DC
BRIAN L. STROM, Rutgers, the State University of New Jersey, Newark
JANET TOBIAS, Ikana Media, New York, NY
JOANNE WALDSTREICHER, Johnson & Johnson, New Brunswick, NJ
JANET WOODCOCK, U.S. Food and Drug Administration, Rockville, MD

IOM Staff

ANNE B. CLAIBORNE, Forum Director
REBECCA A. ENGLISH, Program Officer
CHRISTOPHER J. DEFEO, Program Officer
ELIZABETH F. C. TYSON, Associate Program Officer
BARRET ZIMMERMANN, Senior Program Assistant (until July 2014)
KATHRYN HOWELL, Senior Program Assistant (as of August 2014)
ANDREW M. POPE, Director, Board on Health Sciences Policy

Reviewers

This workshop summary has been reviewed in draft form by individuals chosen for their diverse perspectives and technical expertise, in accordance with procedures approved by the National Research Council's Report Review Committee. The purpose of this independent review is to provide candid and critical comments that will assist the institution in making its published workshop summary as sound as possible and to ensure that the workshop summary meets institutional standards for objectivity, evidence, and responsiveness to the study charge. The review comments and draft manuscript remain confidential to protect the integrity of the process. We wish to thank the following individuals for their review of this workshop summary:

Patricia Furlong, Parent Project Muscular Dystrophy
Elaine K. Gallin, QE Philanthropic Advisors
Robert J. Meyer, University of Virginia School of Medicine
Michael Rosenblatt, Merck & Co., Inc.

Although the reviewers listed above have provided many constructive comments and suggestions, they did not see the final draft of the workshop summary before its release. The review of this workshop summary was overseen by **Eli Y. Adashi,** The Warren Alpert Medical School, Brown University. Appointed by the Institute of Medicine, he was responsible for making certain that an independent examination of this workshop summary was carried out in accordance with institutional procedures and that all review comments were carefully considered. Responsibility for the final content of this workshop summary rests entirely with the rapporteurs and the institution.

Contents

Boxes, Figures, and Table

BOXES

FIGURES

TABLE

Acronyms

AC	advisory committee
BHU	Benefit–Harm–Uncertainty Initiative (Health Canada)
CDER	Center for Drug Evaluation and Research, FDA
COPD	chronic obstructive pulmonary disease
CV	cardiovascular
DRDC	Defence Research and Development Canada
EMA	European Medicines Agency
FDA	U.S. Food and Drug Administration
IMI	Innovative Medicines Initiative
IOM	Institute of Medicine
JCV	John Cunningham virus
LABA	long-acting beta2-adrenergic agonist
LAMA	long-acting antimuscarinic agent
MACE	major adverse cardiac event

MI	myocardial infarction
MS	multiple sclerosis
NEJM	*New England Journal of Medicine*
NIH	National Institutes of Health
PDUFA	Prescription Drug User Fee Act
PFDD	Patient-Focused Drug Development
PML	progressive multifocal leukoencephalopathy
PRO	patient-reported outcome
PROMPT	Prospective Routine Observational Monitoring Program Tools
PROTECT	Pharmacoepidemiological Research on Outcomes of Therapeutics by a European Consortium
RCT	randomized controlled trial
REMS	Risk Evaluation and Mitigation Strategy
SMU	Special Medical Use
SPRC	Stanford Prevention Research Center

1

Introduction[1]

Despite the extensive body of evidence that informs regulatory decisions on pharmaceutical products, significant uncertainties persist, including the underlying variability in human biology, factors associated with the chemistry of a drug, and limitations in the research and clinical trial process itself that might limit the generalizability of results. As a result, regulatory reviewers are consistently required to draw conclusions about a drug's safety and efficacy from imperfect data. Efforts are under way within the drug development community to enhance the evaluation and communication of the benefits and risks associated with pharmaceutical products, aimed at increasing the predictability, transparency, and efficiency of pharmaceutical regulatory decision making. The U.S. Food and Drug Administration (FDA) is developing an enhanced structured approach to benefit–risk assessments[2] in drug regulatory decision making

[1] The planning committee's role was limited to planning the workshop, and the workshop summary has been prepared by the workshop rapporteurs as a factual summary of what occurred at the workshop. Statements, recommendations, and opinions expressed are those of individual presenters and participants, and are not necessarily endorsed or verified by the Forum or the Institute of Medicine, and they should not be construed as reflecting any group consensus.

[2] Terminology in defining benefit–risk assessment varies. Some have indicated the most precise way to reference the separate concepts of benefit and risk, and the different tradeoffs, is to leave the terms unhyphenated because "benefit–risk" assessment could imply reducing benefit and risk to one common metric (as in cost–benefit analysis). Many (e.g., Lim, 2014) suggest the term "benefit–risk" is inconsistent and inherently confusing because risk has a wide range of meanings, noting that a more appropriate term is "benefit–harm"

BOX 1-1[a]
FDA PDUFA V Plan and the Characterization of Uncertainties in Benefits and Risks

The FDA PDUFA V Plan identifies the following two areas of uncertainty as warranting additional attention:

1. *The translation of premarket clinical trial data to the postmarket setting in which an approved drug is used in a much wider patient population.* Several individual workshop participants noted that formal mechanisms could help to assess outcomes for heterogeneous subpopulations that would use the drug differently from patients in clinical trials.
2. *A new finding emerges in a postmarket setting where the basis for the finding comes from sources of varying levels of rigor.* Some individual workshop participants raised questions about how to improve observational studies so that data arising from those studies can be effectively included in the benefit–risk assessment.

[a] This box is based on FDA's PDUFA V Plan (FDA, 2013), material from *Characterizing Uncertainty in the Assessment of Benefits and Risks of Pharmaceutical Products: Workshop in Brief* (IOM, 2014), also prepared for this project, and the remarks and discussions of individuals workshop participants.

to better communicate this aspect of the human drug review process.[3] As FDA has indicated in its draft Prescription Drug User Fee Act (PDUFA) V Implementation Plan (FDA, 2013) (the FDA PDUFA V Plan), identifying and evaluating sources of uncertainty in a regulatory application is an important part of an FDA new drug application reviewers' work; however, drawing conclusions in the face of uncertainty can be a complex and challenging task. Effectively communicating regulatory decisions necessarily includes explanation of the impact of uncertainty on decision making. The FDA PDUFA V Plan suggests that FDA's enhanced structured approach is intended to serve as a template for product reviews and a vehicle to explain the basis of regulatory decisions.[4] Box 1-1 provides additional information on the two areas of uncertainty suggested in the FDA PDUFA V Plan as deserving additional attention.

or "benefit–harm–uncertainty." For this report we have adopted the most widely used "benefit–risk" terminology for ease of reading and because it was the terminology used in defining the workshop charge.

[3] For more information, see http://www.fda.gov/ForIndustry/UserFees/PrescriptionDrugUserFee/ucm326192.htm (accessed August 18, 2014).

[4] This material is based on *Characterizing Uncertainty in the Assessment of Benefits and Risks of Pharmaceutical Products: Workshop in Brief* (IOM, 2014), also prepared for this project.

On February 12 and May 12, 2014, the Institute of Medicine's (IOM's) Forum on Drug Discovery, Development, and Translation (the Forum) held public workshops at FDA Headquarters in White Oak, Maryland, to advance the development of more systematic and structured approaches to characterize and communicate the sources of uncertainty in the assessment of benefits and risks, and to consider their implications for pharmaceutical regulatory decisions (see Box 1-2 for the Statement of Task). Workshop presentations and discussions on February 12 were convened to explore the science of identifying and characterizing uncertainty in scientific evidence and approaches to translate uncertainties into decisions that reflect the values of stakeholders. The May 12 workshop presentations and discussions explored tools and approaches to communicating about scientific uncertainties to a range of stakeholders in the drug development process. Baruch Fischhoff, Howard Heinz University Professor, Department of Social and Decision Sciences, Department of Engineering

BOX 1-2
Statement of Task for the Workshops

An ad hoc planning committee will plan two 1-day public workshops that will address the need to advance the development of more systematic and structured approaches to characterize and communicate: (a) the sources of uncertainty in the assessment of benefits and risks, and (b) their implications on pharmaceutical regulatory decisions. Specifically, the workshops will explore potential analytical and communication approaches and identify key considerations on their development, evaluation, and incorporation into pharmaceutical benefit–risk assessment. Uncertainty in drug review and decision making can arise from many sources. The workshops will consider the entire drug development lifecycle, including premarket drug review and postmarket safety surveillance. Subject-matter experts will be invited to participate in the workshops through presentations and discussions that will:

- Discuss the challenges in applying more systematic approaches to characterizing and communicating uncertainty in the assessment of a drug's benefits and risks.
- Identify potential approaches to characterize uncertainty in pharmaceutical benefit–risk assessment, drawing from various scientific and regulatory disciplines and domains.
- Identify possible principles, best practices, and resources that can facilitate the development, evaluation, and incorporation of such approaches in regulatory decision making.
- Explore principles and approaches to facilitate the communication of uncertainty in benefit–risk assessment to stakeholders, including the public.

and Public Policy, Carnegie Mellon University, and Robert Ratner, Chief Scientific and Medical Officer, American Diabetes Association, were co-chairs of the workshop planning committee. See Box 1-4 at the end of this chapter for themes identified by the workshop co-chairs.

This report is a summary of the February 12 and May 12, 2014, workshops. Statements, recommendations, and opinions expressed are those of individual presenters and participants and are not necessarily endorsed or verified by the Forum or the IOM, and they should not be construed as reflecting any group consensus. The workshops were webcast live, and online participants were able to contribute to discussion through the hashtag #UncertaintyWorkshopIOM. The presentations, videos, and tweets are archived on the Forum websites.[5]

This summary of the workshop is meant to inform FDA; the scientific research community in academia, government, and regulated industry; policy makers; patient groups; the public; and other stakeholders because they all have an interest in the approaches to characterizing and communicating uncertainty in assessments of benefit and risk of pharmaceutical products. The remainder of this first chapter of the summary provides an overview of the role of uncertainty in FDA's benefit–risk framework and compiles a brief overview of themes from the workshop as identified by workshop co-chairs Fischhoff and Ratner. Chapter 2 examines the sources of uncertainty in benefit–risk assessments and opportunities to reduce uncertainty through the clinical research process. Chapter 3 considers the challenges of the pharmaceutical regulator in identifying, acknowledging, addressing, and communicating uncertainties in evidence in the context of FDA's statutory requirements and current efforts to better understand what matters most to patients. Chapter 4 draws on approaches from decision science and statistical techniques to manage uncertainty in the generation of evidence and the regulatory decision-making process. Chapter 5 highlights principles of effective risk communication and potential opportunities to improve the utility of current communication tools and approaches for conveying benefits, risks, and uncertainties to a broad audience, in part through a case study of Tysabri. Chapter 6 concludes this summary of the workshop with views expressed by individual participants during the final workshop session about potential opportunities to move forward in developing approaches for characterizing and communicating uncertainty in the assessments of benefits and risks of pharmaceutical products.

[5] For more information, see http://www.iom.edu/BenefitRisk1 (accessed August 20, 2014) and http://www.iom.edu/BenefitRisk2 (accessed August 20, 2014).

THE IMPACT OF UNCERTAINTY ON REGULATORY DECISION MAKING[6]

When a regulatory decision is made, uncertainty can remain about many aspects of a new drug's performance, said Janet Woodcock, Director, Center for Drug Evaluation and Research (CDER), FDA. As a result, she noted, uncertainty is "central to the evaluation of data," and can affect our understanding of both benefits and risks. Uncertainty in the drug review process has many sources, all of which, she noted, must be analyzed, quantified to the extent possible, judged, and communicated responsibly (see Box 1-3). FDA's goal is to bring the best possible science to bear on these tasks, in order to ensure that stakeholders and the public have a clear understanding of both the available evidence and the pending uncertainties, and that stakeholders understand that both evidence and uncertainty are important factors in any given regulatory decision.

Patrick J. Frey, Director, Office of Program and Strategic Analysis, CDER, FDA, introduced FDA's benefit–risk framework (see Figure 1-1) developed by the agency over several years to delineate the evidence, and accompanying uncertainties, that inform conclusions and decisions about benefits, risks, and the management of risks (e.g., product labeling, Risk Evaluation and Mitigation Strategies, or REMS). Once fully implemented, the framework will serve as both a record of FDA decision making and a tool for communicating the rationale behind regulatory decisions to the public.

FDA currently lacks a systematic approach for dealing with uncertainty, noted Frey. The agency frequently uses advisory committees composed of experts, and in some cases patient representatives, external to government to obtain input on particularly challenging questions about the review of a drug or other issues in drug development and review. The discussions at this workshop are intended by FDA to be the beginning of what will be a multiyear effort by the agency to develop an approach to working through uncertainty that is practical and can be implemented in FDA's unique regulatory setting. Frey noted that FDA is particularly interested in developing systematic approaches to evaluating uncertainty and perhaps exploring the piloting of such systematic approaches in much the same manner as FDA's benefit–risk framework has been piloted.

Several academic disciplines already employ effective approaches to characterizing uncertainty and for supporting decisions made under conditions of uncertainty. Frey noted that adapting existing scientific methods for characterizing and assessing uncertainties can lend additional

[6] This section is based on presentations by Janet Woodcock, Director, CDER, FDA, and Patrick J. Frey, Director, Office of Program and Strategic Analysis, CDER, FDA.

BOX 1-3[a]
The Range of Sources of Uncertainty

Janet Woodcock, Director, CDER, FDA, and Patrick J. Frey, Director, Office of Program and Strategic Analysis, CDER, FDA, presented a range of sources of scientific uncertainty that generally stem from underlying variability in human biology, factors associated with the chemistry of a drug, and the research process:

- ***Human Variability.*** Uncertainties can arise because clinical trials cannot fully represent a drug's effectiveness or harm in more heterogeneous real-world populations.
- ***Clinical Trials.*** The nature of the clinical trial process itself, which is focused on efficacy in a tightly controlled participant population, can give rise to uncertainty. For example, the relatively short duration of a clinical trial leads to uncertainty about long-term effects when the drug will be used chronically in the intended patient population. Limits on the numbers of people assessed in a trial make it difficult to determine whether differences in an adverse effect are real or are "noise." Also, evidence from multiple studies can be inconsistent or contradictory, with no clear way to reconcile results without additional work.
- ***Postmarket Concerns.*** These concerns include the varying levels of rigor in the source of postmarket data (e.g., observational studies, meta-analyses of studies, spontaneous reporting, and active surveillance), as well as the ability of the health care system to manage a "risky" drug.
- ***Unknowns.*** Limits in our scientific understanding of a disease or a physical process make it difficult to know what to investigate and what could be an important "domain of harm" to study. The "unknown unknowns," where researchers do not know what data are missing or are not studied, have historically led to some of the biggest safety controversies, according to Woodcock.

[a] This box is based on presentations by Janet Woodcock, Director, CDER, FDA; Patrick J. Frey, Director, Office of Program and Strategic Analysis, CDER, FDA; and material from *Characterizing Uncertainty in the Assessment of Benefits and Risks of Pharmaceutical Products: Workshop in Brief* (IOM, 2014), also prepared for this project.

intellectual credibility to an activity that is unfamiliar to FDA reviewers who are subject-matter experts. Several practitioners of these methods presented them at the workshop, exploring how they might best support decision makers in areas where evidence is limited.

Decision Factor	Evidence and Uncertainties	Conclusions and Reasons
Analysis of Condition	Summary of evidence:	Conclusions (Implications for decision):
Current Treatment Options	Summary of evidence:	Conclusions (Implications for decision):
Benefit	Summary of evidence:	Conclusions (Implications for decision):
Risk	Summary of evidence:	Conclusions (Implications for decision):
Risk Management	Summary of evidence:	Conclusions (Implications for decision):
Benefit-Risk Summary and Assessment		

Informed by Patient-Focused Drug Development initiative   Informed by IOM workshops

FIGURE 1-1 FDA benefit–risk framework. Color coded areas of the table under the category of "Evidence and Uncertainties" are informed by FDA's Patient-Focused Drug Development initiative and these IOM workshops, respectively.
NOTE: For more information on FDA's benefit–risk framework, see the FDA PDUFA V Plan at: http://www.fda.gov/downloads/forindustry/userfees/prescriptiondruguserfee/ucm329758.pdf (accessed September 12, 2014).
SOURCE: Frey, 2014. Presentation at the IOM workshop series on Characterizing and Communicating Uncertainty in the Assessment of Benefits and Risks of Pharmaceutical Products.

BOX 1-4[a]
Themes Observed by Workshop Co-Chairs

During the course of the February 12 and May 12, 2014, workshop discussions, co-chairs Baruch Fischhoff, Howard Heinz University Professor, Department of Social and Decision Sciences, Department of Engineering and Public Policy, Carnegie Mellon University, and Robert E. Ratner, Chief Scientific and Medical Officer, American Diabetes Association, made observations about themes emerging from speaker presentations and workshop discussions. These themes noted by Fischhoff and Ratner include

- Decision science methods to identify and address uncertainty in the drug review process could make uncertainty "cognitively tractable" in a practical context and be useful to FDA's effort to develop a structured approach to dealing with uncertainty with the benefit–risk framework.
- FDA has a history of being at the forefront of scientific progress and is well suited and well poised to consider and incorporate scientific methods for characterizing uncertainty in the drug review process.
- Systematic approaches and procedures for addressing uncertainty have the promise of improving human judgment, not replacing it.
- In characterizing the value of evidence in the drug review process, it is important to consider the role of outcome measures (e.g., mortality for an acute disease compared to a surrogate outcome for a chronic condition) and their associated uncertainties.
- It could be valuable to offer patients and providers quantified information about benefits, risks, and uncertainties, conveyed in a concise and meaningful way.
- Comparative effectiveness research conducted in real-world patient populations could hold promise for generating the kind of quantitative information to help patients determine the likelihood they will experience a benefit or adverse effect from a drug (i.e., moving beyond mean response data). Developing analytic capabilities to incorporate these types of data in the drug review process and infusing communication strategies with practical information could bring significant benefit to patients and physicians in the decision-making process.
- Once provided information on the benefits and risks of a product, and what is uncertain, unknown, or still being studied, individuals can make informed decisions about their willingness to accept the trade-offs of a treatment based on their unique risk tolerance and personal values.

[a] This box is based on presentations by Baruch Fischhoff, Howard Heinz University Professor, Department of Social and Decision Sciences, Department of Engineering and Public Policy, Carnegie Mellon University, and Robert E. Ratner, Chief Scientific and Medical Officer, American Diabetes Association.

2

Identifying and Characterizing Uncertainty

Key Messages Identified by Individual Speakers

- Benefit–risk assessments are dynamic by nature because the information itself changes over time.
- The goal of a systematic approach to uncertainty might be to improve human judgment, not to automate the process of benefit–risk assessment.
- Several dimensions of uncertainty are inherent to population-based benefit–risk assessments, and operational factors can exacerbate them.
- Finding an approach that can combine results of studies with different designs and data sources might provide a clearer picture of benefits and risks and reduce uncertainty.
- Benefit–risk assessments reflect an interaction among multiple streams of evidence with many stakeholders; understanding the context for each type of evidence could be valuable to the drug evaluation process.
- Stakeholder consultation could help regulators avoid conflating uncertainty regarding the extent of the risk with the willingness to accept that risk.

The first session of the workshop explored several dimensions of the drug decision-making process, examining the sources and types of uncertainties in the research process and how they might relate to, and affect, each other. Speakers from academic research institutions, federal government, and the pharmaceutical industry proposed several principles and approaches to improve the quality of, and reduce the uncertainty associated with, clinical study data. These approaches included finding a scientifically acceptable method to bridge the gap between randomized trials, which focus on proving drug efficacy in a study population, and observational studies, which focus on risk and adverse events in the real world.

KEY SOURCES OF UNCERTAINTY IN BENEFIT–RISK ASSESSMENT AND ASSOCIATED CHALLENGES[1]

Tarek A. Hammad, Executive Director, Epidemiology, Merck Research Laboratories, Merck & Co., Inc., provided an overview of the sources of uncertainty in the benefit–risk assessment process. Noting that the common interest of all stakeholders is to understand the causal effects of a given drug, he observed that the challenge for decision making is to make the best possible judgment about how to value study data. This judgment has inherent qualitative and quantitative components, and includes the understanding that benefit–risk assessment is dynamic and that there are clear imbalances in the sources, timing, and nature of information available throughout a drug's lifecycle (Hammad et al., 2013). For instance, the evidence informing a benefit–risk assessment at the time of approval is limited to tightly controlled randomized controlled trials (RCTs) that are highly reliable for the population being studied, but do not include, by design, categories of patients that will ultimately take a drug. After market approval, once a drug is used in a larger and more diverse population, data about a drug's effects will arise from sources of varied quality and reliability. As time passes, more information is accrued; including, in particular, safety and adverse event data. If data about efficacy and benefit are not accrued in a timely manner during the postmarket period, the benefit–risk profile will appear to be getting worse over time (Hammad et al., 2013).

According to Hammad, the core uncertainty in the drug review process is that benefit–risk assessments rely on data that represent a group

[1] This section is based on the presentation by Tarek A. Hammad, Executive Director, Epidemiology, Merck Research Laboratories, Merck & Co., Inc.

experience, not the effect of a drug on an individual patient. He outlined three distinct, but interrelated, components of uncertainty in evidence.[2]

The first component, *clinical uncertainty*, is a function of the research process itself. For example, RCTs by definition must minimize biological variables in the study population, such as age, gender, genetic profiles, and other health issues or treatments. This reduces the value of RCT results outside the trial population. Also, the standard length of a clinical trial is generally too brief to anticipate adverse events with long latency periods, such as in drugs that treat chronic conditions.

The second component, *methodological uncertainties*, is represented by the fact that RCT methods are tightly constrained to establish evidence in the premarket setting (Hammad et al., 2011), while observational studies are generally employed after the drug is approved to assess real-world risks. Additionally, some RCT methods that are intended to improve trial efficiency might be associated with a reduced ability to characterize all risks, such as randomized withdrawal designs (Hammad et al., 2011).

Statistical uncertainty arises because clinical trials for drug approval are designed to show that a drug works as intended, by evaluating the incremental difference in efficacy between a drug and a comparator, but not necessarily to quantify benefits and risks. In addition, clinical trials involve sampling which, by its nature, introduces the potential for error and thus uncertainty.

Hammad also described a fourth, crosscutting dimension in benefit–risk assessments: *operational uncertainty*. One component is the challenge and need for making postmarket studies part of the overall research process, given that RCT participants are volunteers and cannot be compelled to participate after a drug has been approved. Also, he noted, benefit–risk assessments do not include discussions to establish a "threshold of risk tolerance" that could differ among stakeholders with varying interests (e.g., regulators vs. payers vs. health care providers vs. patients).

The potential for "confounding by information" on the assessment of benefit–risk balance also exists. For instance, health care practitioners might change their practices based on uncertain information in the public domain, which might hinder efforts to fully evaluate the benefit–risk profile based on observational data (Hammad et al., 2013). Finally, population-based surveillance efforts that might be initiated to mitigate uncertainties are constrained by biases and shortcomings, including a lack of effective infrastructure to make the best use of electronic health records and "big data" associated with drug studies.

According to Hammad, the current regulatory approach to dealing with uncertainty is a version of the precautionary principle; that is, regu-

[2] Classification adopted from Berlin et al., 2012.

lators refrain from taking action when the impact of an uncertain hazard is "morally unacceptable." Hammad suggested that there are public health consequences to risk aversion, such as denying market access for a drug that could be beneficial or withdrawing a drug from the market or restricting its use when it could provide more benefit than harm (Eichler et al., 2013). Also, from the patient perspective, overadherence to precaution might be conflating two sources of uncertainty: the uncertainty about *the extent of the risk* with uncertainty about *the willingness of the patient to accept the risk*. Hammad explained that a patient's willingness to accept risk is likely to change over time depending on stage of life and severity of disease, which adds to the complexity of drug regulatory decisions. Hammad suggested five considerations and principles to potentially inform the development of a systematic approach to addressing uncertainty (see Box 2-1).

REDUCING UNCERTAINTY THROUGH MAXIMIZING THE VALUE OF EVIDENCE[3]

Two presenters focused on the quality of evidence available for regulatory decisions: trial registration and participant retention.

Deborah A. Zarin, Director, ClinicalTrials.gov, National Library of Medicine, National Institutes of Health, noted that wide public registration of clinical trials, including results and key protocol details, would support the best possible evidence-based decision making. However, she said, not all clinical trials are registered, and not all registered trials can be found. Trials are often registered under names other than those provided in a new drug application, causing these trials to be "invisible" to registry search engines.

Suboptimal participant retention, with resultant missing data, is a long-standing challenge that can contribute to uncertainty in reviewing clinical trial data, because losing participants during the conduct of a clinical trial skews results in unpredictable ways. Michaela Kiernan, Senior Research Scientist, Stanford Prevention Research Center (SPRC), Stanford University School of Medicine, presented one promising innovative retention approach that could help to optimize both high and non-differential retention of subgroups. An ongoing weight loss study at SPRC involves educating potential participants prior to randomization about research

[3] This section is based on presentations by Deborah A. Zarin, Director, ClinicalTrials.gov, National Library of Medicine, National Institutes of Health; Michaela Kiernan, Senior Research Scientist, Stanford Prevention Research Center (SPRC), Stanford University School of Medicine; and material from *Characterizing Uncertainty in the Assessment of Benefits and Risks of Pharmaceutical Products: Workshop in Brief* (IOM, 2014), also prepared for this project.

BOX 2-1[a]
Considerations for Designing an Approach to Addressing Uncertainty

Preserve the Role of Human Judgment

- Systematizing approaches to uncertainty is meant to improve human judgment, not to replace it with an automated process.

Acknowledge the Complexity of the Decision-Making Process

- Context matters: The same set of facts can lead to a different course of action, depending on the decision maker and the unique situation presented by each product.
- Sources of uncertainty (e.g., clinical, methodological, and statistical) are exacerbated by operational challenges.
- Benefit–risk assessment has inherent qualitative and quantitative components to be taken into consideration.

Understand the Dynamic Nature of Benefit–Risk Assessments

- Clear imbalances exist in the sources, timing, and nature of information on benefit and risk.

Listen to the Patient Perspective

- Benefit–risk assessments could benefit from better ways to characterize and incorporate patient perspectives and preferences throughout the lifecycle of a drug.

Identify and Address Knowledge Gaps

- Addressing known shortcomings in study data can improve decision making under uncertainty.

[a] This section is based on the presentation by Tarek A. Hammad, Executive Director, Epidemiology, Merck Research Laboratories, Merck & Co., Inc.

methods, trial design, control conditions, random assignments, and the impact of dropouts.

METHODS TO ADDRESS UNCERTAINTY IN THE POSTMARKET PHASE[4]

A widely recognized challenge in drug decision making is how to incorporate results from postmarket observational studies with clinical

[4] This section is based on the presentation by Sebastian Schneeweiss, Professor of Medicine and Epidemiology, Harvard Medical School.

trial data. Sebastian Schneeweiss, Professor of Medicine and Epidemiology, Harvard Medical School, noted three main sources of uncertainty in drug studies in the pre- and postmarket phase: chance, bias, and representativeness. Chance and bias (e.g., confounding, time-related biases, surveillance bias, and misclassification) affect internal validity. Chance is addressed through calculation of 95 percent confidence intervals. Bias is addressed through various design and analytic approaches such as negative control outcomes, emulating trial populations, extensive adjustment procedures, bias modeling, and sensitivity analyses. Representativeness affects external validity and can be partially addressed in RCTs through evaluation of subgroups.

Schneeweiss noted that in general, sources of uncertainty vary between RCTs and observational studies and also differently affect the assessment of benefits and harms. RCTs are typically the source for information about benefit or efficacy, while large observational claims data studies are typically the source for information about adverse events in real-world populations.

To collectively provide the most valid, comprehensive, and affordable information for decision makers, Schneeweiss said, a benefit–risk assessment should include evidence from multiple study types with different data sources, intelligently arranged to maximize information available to a decision maker while complementing each study's methodological weaknesses.

He proposed an optimal framework for these interlocking RCT and observational studies, designed to reduce uncertainty and to complement each other in speed, validity, precision, and generalizability (see Figure 2-1). Conducting multiple studies in a cohesive manner can effectively retain patient populations across study designs to gather essential information on benefits and harms that would not be possible in an RCT or observational study alone.

Monitoring settings, such as the Mini-Sentinel surveillance system developed by FDA and its partners, illuminate the need for formal approaches to assessing benefits and harms, according to Schneeweiss. Broad population-based systems that monitor the safety of drugs require the upfront creation of clear decision rules that govern when the information gathered rises to the level of requiring a safety alert to the public. False signals on the safety of a drug—either failing to identify a safety concern or identifying a purported safety issue that is not real—are equally problematic. In the first case, patients would be exposed to unnecessary risk and in the second case, unwarranted concerns would be raised and a safe medication underused. A single probability (p-value) or predefined threshold underlying a decision rule does not adequately consider the balance of benefits and harms for a particular medicine. Schneeweiss

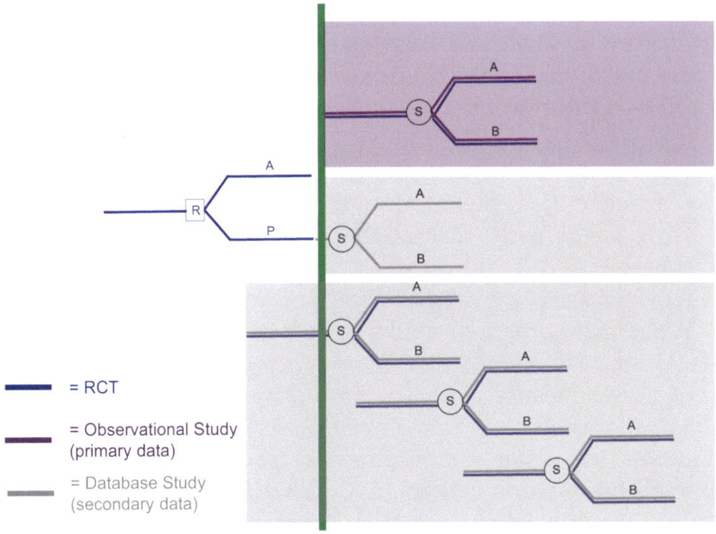

FIGURE 2-1 A system of proactively, prospectively designed interlocking randomized controlled trial (RCT) and observational studies to reduce uncertainty, retain patient populations, and gather information that would not be possible in an RCT or observational study alone.
NOTES: A = drug A; B = drug B; P = placebo; R = randomization; and S = selection. The green vertical line indicates the time of market authorization for a drug. The RCT conducted prior to market authorization would include health claims or electronic health record data for all trial participants prior to the start of the trial. Obtaining these data, with the permission of patients, facilitates the characterization of the RCT patient population via the same data source used in a later observational study, thereby maintaining the comparability of subgroups across study design. Identifying a subgroup within the observational study that mimics the original RCT study population will help to tackle the issue of representativeness and reduce uncertainty. The observational studies suggested in the figure indicate three unique designs: (1) one observational study with primary data (purple shaded area) in which an RCT-like subgroup is identified in a cohort study with primary data in order to reproduce RCT findings to calibrate observational findings in the postmarket setting; (2) one observational follow-on study (middle shaded area) in which the RCT placebo group is retained and self-selects to receive drug A or drug B, thereby assessing a non-randomized finding in the original RCT population; and (3) a monitoring system of sequential observational database studies that maintain an RCT-like patient subgroup that mimics the original trial population over time. The combined effect of these studies is to provide valid and comprehensive information for benefit and risk decision makers in an integrated and cost-effective manner.
SOURCE: Schneeweiss, 2014. Presentation at the IOM workshop series on Characterizing and Communicating Uncertainty in the Assessment of Benefits and Risks of Pharmaceutical Products.

suggested that decision rules for safety monitoring systems should incorporate decision-analytic and value-of-information approaches that would allow monitoring decisions to be made over time and incorporate answers to the following questions:

- What is the availability of an alternative drug?
- How effective is the monitored drug compared to an alternative?
- How severe is the disease that the drug treats (e.g., skin rash vs. cancer)?
- How severe is the safety concern of interest?
- What is the prognosis of the population without any treatment?

Many of these questions require significant decision-maker input and might vary by population. Schneeweiss asserted that epidemiologic studies or monitoring systems should be constructed to provide the relevant information for decision makers (e.g., risk differences, not only ratios) as validly as possible. Mini-Sentinel's Prospective Routine Observational Monitoring Program Tools (PROMPT) modules consisting of preprogrammed and tested analytic code that is applied to an existing common data model can provide this in an expedited manner (Gagne et al., 2014).

APPROACHES TO ASSESSING INTERNAL AND EXTERNAL VALIDITY OF RCTs[5]

John P. A. Ioannidis, C. F. Rehnborg Professor in Disease Prevention, Stanford University; and Professor of Health Research and Policy, and Director of SPRC, Stanford University School of Medicine, presented results from approaches he has used to assess the internal and external validity of RCTs.

When trials have design flaws, their effect sizes can be exaggerated. One study (Savovic et al., 2012) combined data from nearly 2,000 RCTs with the goal of ascertaining the influence of reported study design characteristics on intervention effect estimates. Study design characteristics included generation of randomization sequence, allocation concealment, and blinding (or not). On average, Ioannidis said, trials that do not have clear generation of their randomization sequence, or have inadequate or unclear allocation concealment, tend to have inflated effect sizes compared to those that do. The difference is about 10 percent on a relative scale, but, he noted, it can make a big difference depending on the out-

[5] This section is based on the presentation by John P. A. Ioannidis, C. F. Rehnborg Professor in Disease Prevention, Stanford University; and Professor of Health Research and Policy, and Director of SPRC, Stanford University School of Medicine.

come of interest (e.g., mortality or another objective outcome compared to something that is subjective). Mortality, he observed, seemed to be least affected by study design. Subjective outcomes tend to be affected the most by the validity of study design, ranging from 20 to 30 percent.

As some workshop participants had also noted, Ioannidis argued that to address external generalizability, a trial needs to be compared against other trials done in the same field on questions that are relevant. He emphasized that the outcomes of interest are whether one drug is better than another (rather than a placebo) and the relative uncertainty of one drug versus another.

3

The Regulators' Challenge

Key Messages Identified by Individual Speakers

- FDA's analysis of benefits and risks of pharmaceutical products is supported by an extensive body of evidence and analyzed through the lens of science, medicine, policy, values, and judgment—yet uncertainties persist about products under review.
- All scientific evidence is not created equal. Evidence facing a reviewer at the time of a marketing decision is largely designed to show a product's efficacy, or benefit. Adverse events are usually found in postmarket, observational settings.
- Canadian regulators are working to incorporate transparency about the benefit, harm, and uncertainty considerations in regulatory decisions, with the goal of aligning decisions and accompanying communication strategies to better serve patients.
- Developing an understanding of what matters most to patients could help FDA craft regulatory decisions and outreach that meaningfully communicates uncertain issues in a manner most relevant to patients.

Patrick Frey, CDER, FDA, referred to FDA's multidimensional approach to benefit–risk assessment to frame the challenges that uncertainty poses for regulators. Frey said these assessments, which are the foundation for drug approval decisions, are supported by an extensive body of evidence, informed by the underlying disease and available treatment options, and analyzed through the lens of science, medicine, policy, values, and judgment. Yet uncertainties persist, relating both to the benefits and the risks of products under review.

Although the decision points themselves might be unique to the drug review process, the types of uncertainties that underlie them could be better characterized and addressed by scientific methods that support decision making under uncertainty. For example, Frey noted, establishing predictive expertise in scientifically analyzing uncertainty can be difficult, especially for a process like a drug review, which is driven by scientific evidence. Even though uncertainties exist, reviewers with clinical and regulatory expertise do not typically make explicit the assumptions that might be inherent in dealing with uncertainty in decision making. Furthermore, hypothetical questioning, which could be used to aid in thinking through a decision under uncertainty, is not typical practice in an evidence-driven organization like FDA, noted Frey. A method from the field of decision science, expert elicitation, could be used to guide experts through a process by which their informed opinions on a given area of uncertainty can be synthesized and perhaps even quantified in a way that reveals that uncertainty. Frey indicated that expert elicitation methods might be applicable in the drug regulatory setting, allowing FDA drug reviewers to participate in a process that has been effective for quantifying uncertainty in other areas. Frey noted that such decision science methods have potential in the drug regulatory setting for developing a systematic approach to uncertainty that is both scientifically rigorous and can be practically implemented in FDA's existing benefit–risk framework.

Francesco Pignatti, Head of Oncology, Hematology, Diagnostics Section, Scientific and Regulatory Management Department, Human Medicines Evaluation Division, European Medicines Agency (EMA), cited parallel efforts in Europe to develop a structured approach to benefit–risk assessments and particularly to further develop the methods and tools that characterize and mitigate uncertainty. Pignatti and Kimby Barton, Director, Bureau of Cardiology, Allergy and Neurological Sciences, Health Canada, indicated that a goal of European and Canadian regulators is also to increase transparency of benefit–risk assessments and explicitly link evaluations of uncertainty with a particular remediating action (i.e., designing a new study, developing a new label to reflect uncertainty, or requiring the development of a risk management system).

UNIQUE CHALLENGES OF THE PHARMACEUTICAL REGULATORY SETTING[1]

Baruch Fischhoff, Carnegie Mellon University, reflected on FDA's efforts to build a benefit–risk framework that quantifies the risks and benefits of a product to the greatest extent possible, but without losing the uncertainties and the context that allow for nuanced interpretation of what is known and what else we would like to know. Fischhoff observed that FDA has separated scientific judgment from regulatory interpretation in the benefit–risk framework, but allowed the acknowledgment of uncertainty throughout the process of assessing benefits and risks. The fact that FDA has not sought a common metric to assess benefit or risk, or both together, but has chosen to treat them as independent variables not to be combined so that each can be characterized in its own right, is, according to Fischhoff, the appropriate approach to inform the regulatory decision maker.

Challenges Facing the Regulator in Communicating Uncertainties in Risks of Approved Products[2]

Mary H. Parks, Deputy Director, Office of Drug Evaluation II, Office of New Drugs, CDER, FDA, spoke about the uncertainties inherent in the interpretation of scientific evidence in the drug review process, and how those uncertainties are communicated both within the agency and outside.

The FDA PDUFA V Plan states: "To be approved for marketing, a drug must be safe and effective for its intended use." Parks emphasized that the statement does not mean that an approved drug is risk free. Instead, the statement indicates that FDA, based on its review of scientific evidence, has determined that the benefits of a drug outweigh its risks when used as directed.

As "scientific evidence" is the determining factor for drug approvals, Parks posed three questions to highlight the nuances inherent in the term:

1. How is scientific evidence defined?
2. Is all scientific evidence created equal?
3. When different people look at the same scientific evidence, will they come to the same conclusion?

---

[1] This section is based on the presentation by Baruch Fischhoff, Howard Heinz University Professor, Department of Social and Decision Sciences, Department of Engineering and Public Policy, Carnegie Mellon University.

[2] This subsection is based on the presentation by Mary H. Parks, Deputy Director, Office of Drug Evaluation II, Office of New Drugs, CDER, FDA.

Defining Scientific Evidence

Parks noted that what FDA can treat as scientific evidence is defined by federal statute. Section 505(d) of the federal Food, Drug, and Cosmetic Act defines *substantial evidence* as:

> evidence consisting of adequate and well-controlled investigations, including clinical investigations, by experts qualified by scientific training and experience to evaluate the effectiveness of the drug involved, on the basis of which it could fairly and responsibly be concluded by such experts that the drug will have the effect it purports or is represented to have under the conditions of use prescribed, recommended, or suggested in the labeling or proposed labeling thereof.

Parks emphasized that this definition applies only to evidence that is used to determine a drug's effectiveness. No legal standard currently exists to define "substantial evidence" for safety determinations.

Not All Scientific Evidence Is Created Equal

A ranking system for scientific evidence has been in use for many years, based on the rigor of the methods used to produce it (see Table 3-1).

TABLE 3-1 Hierarchy of Scientific Evidence

Level	Type of Scientiic Evidence
Ia	Scientific evidence obtained from meta-analyses of randomized clinical trials
Ib	Scientific evidence obtained from at least one randomized clinical trial
IIa	Scientific evidence obtained from at least one well-designed, non-randomized controlled prospective study
IIb	Scientific evidence obtained from at least one well-designed, quasi-experimental study
III	Scientific evidence obtained from well-designed observational studies, such as comparative studies, correlation study, or case-control studies
IV	Scientific evidence obtained from documents or opinions of experts, committees, and/or clinical experiences of renowned opinion leaders

NOTES: Category Ib, scientific evidence from at least one randomized clinical trial (RCT), is used in drug trials. Workshop participants also discussed opportunities to gather important benefit and harm information from prospectively planned RCTs for regulatory approval as well as observational studies conducted after a product is used widely by patients in the real world.
SOURCE: Parks, 2014. Presentation at the IOM workshop series on Characterizing and Communicating Uncertainty in the Assessment of Benefits and Risks of Pharmaceutical Products.

A drug trial collects evidence to support efficacy, which when done through an RCT, yields the highest level of evidence. Sponsors prospectively design RCTs with a specific efficacy endpoint in mind, often with input from FDA scientists.

In contrast, safety data rarely come from prospectively designed, controlled trials. Indeed, obtaining the "signal of concern" about an adverse outcome is one of the most difficult issues that drug regulators face. The RCT does not serve as the same gold standard in safety as in efficacy. Most RCTs are not designed to prospectively look for safety concerns and, as a result, any safety data collected are likely to be insufficient.

More often, as noted by Parks and other workshop participants, potential harms or adverse events are generally found in postmarket, observational study data, or via other methods that are considered less rigorous than RCTs, but that can reveal important safety information that is more relevant to patients outside the restricted RCT population.

Same Evidence, Different Reviewers, Different Conclusions

Drug reviewers must analyze many lines of data that might vary in quality, noted Parks. As a result, they often adopt different interpretations of the reviewed evidence.

Parks indicated that difficult drug applications, where there are substantive disagreements among reviewers about safety and risk, are not simply passed along for a signatory authority to review and decide. Before a final decision is made, internal and external risk communication procedures, including the agency's safety committees, ensure that offices throughout the agency are involved in helping to resolve the issues. Box 3-1 lists FDA's procedures that can be deployed in the drug review context to inform risk communication.

COMMUNICATING WITH THE PUBLIC ABOUT BENEFIT, HARM, AND UNCERTAINTY[3]

Robyn Lim, Senior Science Advisor, Office of Legislative and Regulatory Modernization, Health Products and Food Branch, Health Canada, presented Health Canada's Benefit–Harm–Uncertainty Initiative (BHU), a new regulatory approach focused on communication and patients. BHU is directing increasing attention to patients in order to help them understand the role of uncertainty in the real-world decisions they need to make about

[3] This section is based on the presentation by Robyn Lim, Senior Science Advisor, Office of Legislative and Regulatory Modernization, Health Products and Food Branch, Health Canada.

BOX 3-1[a]
FDA Approaches to Inform Risk Communication

Internal Procedures

- FDA review template (benefit–risk framework)
- Briefings (intra/interoffice, regulatory, Center Director)
- Committees (REMS oversight, Safety First Steering Committee)

External Procedures

- Drug Safety Oversight Board (federal partners)
- Advisory Committee Meetings (external scientific experts)
- Published perspectives
- Outreach (medical community, Patient Focused Drug Development Initiative)

---

[a] This box is based on the presentation by Mary H. Parks, Deputy Director, Office of Drug Evaluation II, Office of New Drugs, CDER, FDA.

treatment options. Health Canada is modernizing its regulatory approach to drug approval by "hard-wiring" communication about uncertainty into federal legislation. The new system will include mandated transparency about the benefit, harm, and uncertainty considerations in regulatory decisions with the goal of aligning regulatory decisions and accompanying communication strategies to better serve the needs of health partners, particularly patients.

The guiding principle behind BHU, according to Lim, is that pairing the terms "benefit" and "risk" is inherently confusing because there is an asymmetrical acknowledgment of uncertainty in the terms, and that confusion undermines patients' ability to think about choices and trade-offs in a disciplined way. The definition of *benefit* does not include the concept of uncertainty, Lim said, while *risk* has a wide ranging set of definitions. Definitions of risk include the possibility that something bad or unpleasant can happen, or a "hazard," with the possibility of both chance and uncertainty.

As a result, Lim said, tolerance for risk is usually interpreted as tolerance for a harm or hazardous outcome. However, she noted, tolerance for risk is not the same as tolerance for uncertainty. Tolerance for risk is accepting the possibility of harm, while tolerance for uncertainty includes the acceptance of a much broader scope of possible outcomes—that, for better or worse, uncertainty can exist within stated benefits as well as potential hazards, and other outcomes as well.

During fall 2014, Health Canada is finishing the final draft of its *Patient's Decision Guide About Treatments,* a structured, step-wise process that provides patients with a simple, methodical way to think about positive effects, negative effects, and uncertainties of treatments, so they can make better informed decisions.

FDA Patient-Focused Drug Development Initiative[4]

Patients are uniquely positioned to inform FDA's understanding of the clinical context for a disease or condition. Having an understanding of what matters most to patients, including what they want and need to know, helps inform the agency's regulatory decisions and outreach that meaningfully communicate uncertain issues in a manner most relevant to patients, noted Theresa Mullin, Director, Office of Strategic Programs, CDER, FDA. While FDA has a number of mechanisms to obtain patient input,[5] it is typically limited to discussions related to issues associated with a particular product or class of products. The Patient-Focused Drug Development (PFDD) initiative[6] is different because it is more broadly focused and systematic, and does not focus on a single product.

PFDD operates by providing patients with an in-person forum for discussion about the impact of a specific condition or disease on their daily lives, and the treatment options that are available to them. According to Mullin, the PFDD initiative was the result of agency thinking about limitations in the information and the sources of information available for consideration in a drug review.

For a drug to be approved for marketing, FDA must determine that the drug is effective and that its benefits outweigh its risks. The agency wanted to undertake a more systematic approach to gathering patient input to inform this benefit–risk assessment, particularly the therapeutic context concerning the severity of the disease condition and the degree to which current therapies are meeting patients' needs (see Figure 1-1 and remarks by Frey). PFDD gives the agency the opportunity to hear from patients directly and gather important input on what it is like to live with the disease, their experience with current treatment options, and what they look for in an ideal treatment. Although uncertainty is not the main focus for PFDD meetings, Mullin noted that patients often must

---

[4] This subsection is based on the presentation by Theresa Mullin, Director, Office of Strategic Programs, CDER, FDA.

[5] FDA patient engagement tools include FDA Patient Representative Program; Patient Consultant Program; Patient Liaison and Patient Network programs; and CDER's Professional Affairs and Stakeholder Engagement.

[6] For more information about Patient-Focused Drug Development (PFDD) and the at least 20 disease-focused meetings FDA has committed to conducting in 2013–2017, as a result of PDUFA V, see http://www.fda.gov/ForIndustry/UserFees/PrescriptionDrugUserFee/ucm347317.htm (accessed August 8, 2014).

BOX 3-2[a]
Exploring Patient Perspectives on Uncertainty Through PFDD

Although not the main focus, issues of uncertainty often are addressed at PFDD meetings. Two examples:

- For HIV: Emerging "cure research" is essential for advancing drug development, but the risks of experimental therapies, such as gene therapy, are highly uncertain.
  - What factors do patients take into account when considering whether to participate in a research study?
  - How should the uncertainties about the study's benefits and risks be communicated through the informed consent process?
- For lung cancer: The benefits of cancer treatments to an individual patient can be highly uncertain.
  - What are patients' priorities, particularly with respect to prolonging life vs. preserving quality of life?
  - How might patients' priorities change as their situations change?

---

[a] This box is based on the presentation by Theresa Mullin, Director, Office of Strategic Programs, CDER, FDA.

consider scientific uncertainty, for example, when considering whether to take a treatment or participate in a clinical trial. PFDD meetings present an opportunity for agency reviewers to engage patients in discussion about the factors that weigh into these decisions and what information they want to know about benefits, risks, and uncertainties (see Box 3-2).

According to Mullin, input from patients to date has been very useful for FDA reviewers, who will conduct future benefit–risk assessments for drugs to treat specific diseases. Patient discussions and conversations strengthen the agency's understanding of the relative importance of clinical outcomes, and what types of risks might be considered acceptable to patients. Patient input could also support drug development more broadly, for instance, by identifying specific symptoms, such as fatigue, that are not being remedied by current treatment options. The formation of an interested and informed patient community could also support the identification and development of a process to collect patient-reported outcome[7] (PRO) measures.

Mullin also elaborated on ways that patient communities not represented in the original 20 disease-focused meetings scheduled through 2017 might conduct their own similar meetings to inform the agency of what matters most to patients with a particular disease or condition. The PFDD meetings currently organized by FDA follow a consistent format and all meeting materials, as well as the final summary reports, are publicly available. Mullin noted that hosting meetings in the Washington area, and generally in close proximity to Silver Spring or Bethesda, would facilitate attendance by FDA staff.

To provide context for workshop discussions surrounding regulatory decision making under uncertainty, FDA developed two case studies to illustrate the types of uncertainties that FDA reviewers face in weighing the evidence for a particular product to receive market approval (see Box 3-3 and Appendix B for complete case studies).

[7] A patient-reported outcome is any report of the status of a patient's health condition that comes directly from the patient, without interpretation of the patient's response by a clinician or anyone else. Additional information is available here: http://www.fda.gov/downloads/Drugs/Guidances/UCM193282.pdf (accessed September 8, 2014).

BOX 3-3[a]
Decisions Made Under Uncertainty: Tysabri and Anoro Ellipta Case Studies

Patrick J. Frey, Director, Office of Program and Strategic Analysis, CDER, FDA, provided an overview of FDA's approach to evaluating benefits and risks of pharmaceutical products, with specific focus on how these approaches take sources of uncertainty into consideration. The FDA PDUFA V Plan notes that systematic approaches to evaluating uncertainty is an area worthy of further consideration to inform the drawing of conclusions in the context of uncertainty. Frey stated that FDA is interested in exploring a systematic approach to uncertainty, much like the benefit–risk framework. FDA developed two case studies to illustrate the types of complex uncertainties that FDA reviewers must address when making decisions based on clinical evidence. These case studies were prepared and presented to describe real-life examples of uncertainty that a regulator faces to illuminate evaluation of uncertainty in assessment of the benefits and risks through the eyes of a regulator. The case studies can be accessed in Appendix B of this report as well as at the meeting website.[b]

Tysabri (natalizumab). Robert Temple, Deputy Director for Clinical Science, and Acting Deputy Director, Office of Drug Evaluation I, CDER, FDA, described the Tysabri case study. Four months after its initial approval to treat patients with multiple sclerosis (MS), Tysabri (natalizumab) was withdrawn from the market because two patients died after developing a life-threatening, often fatal, brain infection called progressive multifocal leukoencephalopathy (PML). At the time, there was considerable uncertainty about the magnitude of the risk of PML to patients exposed to Tysabri and whether there were any identifiable risk factors that could reliably identify patients at greater risk. In determining whether to allow remarketing of the drug, FDA considered whether the risk of PML (and uncertainty about the risk) outweighed the drug's recognized substantial benefit. The agency examined additional data provided by the company developing the drug and consulted with an advisory committee that included patients with MS. Temple noted that while patients plainly understood the risk that contracting PML could be fatal, they provided "powerful personal testimony" in favor of reintroducing Tysabri. In response, FDA allowed marketing of Tysabri to resume, accompanied by an extensive risk mitigation plan that included requirements for strict labeling and safety information; controlled distribution; and a prospective, observational postmarketing study, following at least 5,000 patients for 5 years.

Anoro Ellipta. The case study on Anoro Ellipta (umeclidinium and vilanterol inhalation powder) was outlined by Jennifer R. Pippins, Medical Officer, Division of Pulmonary, Allergy, and Rheumatology Products, Office of New Drugs, CDER, FDA. In December 2013, FDA approved Anoro Ellipta as a long-term maintenance treatment for patients with chronic obstructive pulmonary disease. One of its agents, umeclidinium, is a member of a class of long-acting agents that have been the subject of concern since 2007, when pooled analyses suggested increased cardiovascular (CV) risks associated with another drug in the same class. The low numbers of major cardiac events in Anoro Ellipta's premarket clinical trials made it difficult to draw definitive conclusions about CV risk. According to Pippins, FDA's view was that the observational studies the sponsor proposed would not be able to provide a definitive assessment of cardiac risk; as a result, the agency decided not to require postmarket monitoring.

---

[a] This box is based on remarks from Patrick J. Frey, Director, Office of Program and Strategic Analysis, CDER, FDA; Robert Temple, Deputy Director for Clinical Science, and Acting Deputy Director, Office of Drug Evaluation I, CDER, FDA; Jennifer R. Pippins, Medical Officer, Division of Pulmonary, Allergy, and Rheumatology Products, Office of New Drugs, CDER, FDA; and material from *Characterizing Uncertainty in the Assessment of Benefits and Risks of Pharmaceutical Products: Workshop in Brief* (IOM, 2014), also prepared for this project.

[b] See Appendix B or the meeting website: http://www.iom.edu/BenefitRisk1 (accessed April 2, 2014).

4

Basic Methodologies and Applications for Understanding and Evaluating Uncertainty

Key Messages Identified by Individual Speakers

- Expert elicitation can be applied to issues of uncertainty, allowing the incorporation of informal evidence that contributes to the expert's judgment alongside formal evidence.
- Eliciting values for risk governance choices is a process of applying structured common sense to complex problems.
- Language can be limited in its ability to convey accurate information. Making clear to the reader what information is known with certainty and what is reasoned judgment could help address these limitations.
- The valuation process for managing risk includes both technical (scientific) information and value-based information (preferences) to clarify and examine trade-offs.
- Bayesian approaches to evaluating clinical trial data have the potential to facilitate more robust characterization of inferences drawn from studies.

APPLYING DECISION SCIENCE IN THE DRUG REVIEW PROCESS

Several presenters discussed the merit of using judgment and decision science to address uncertainty in the drug review process. Its methods, they stated, serve to make uncertainty tractable, providing a practical context for considering the value of evidence and revealing important new uncertainties that might otherwise have been overlooked.

Eliciting Expert Judgment[1]

A technique called *expert elicitation* uses a one-on-one interview process to seek expert input about topics where there are insufficient data or where data are unattainable. According to M. Granger Morgan, Professor and Head of the Department of Engineering and Public Policy, Carnegie Mellon University, the elicitation process draws out carefully reasoned, individual judgments, then summarizes the results of several interviews to provide an indication of the range of expert views and associated uncertainty, usually in the form of subjective probability distributions.

A key benefit offered by expert elicitation is that informal evidence that contributes to the expert's judgment can be incorporated together with formal evidence, said Morgan. Expert elicitation can be applied to uncertainty not only about a quantity or mathematical probability, but also about a process or a model function. For example, as suggested by one workshop participant, an expert elicitation in the drug review process might quantify expert judgment about the relative likelihood that alternative models of pharmacokinetic or pharmacodynamic processes correctly describe a given biological process.

Morgan provided three cautions with respect to the application of expert elicitation: (1) only those with relevant expertise should be interviewed, in order to ensure that judgments obtained are well informed; (2) words that are used to describe uncertainty, such as "likely" and "unlikely," should be quantified, because they often mean different things to different people, or even to the same people in different situations; and (3) cognitive biases inherent to human judgment can affect experts' responses. Morgan described two of the most frequently occurring biases, "availability" and "anchoring and adjustment."

Availability

Morgan noted that people tend to estimate the frequency of an event by how quickly or easily they can recall or imagine similar instances or occurrences. The "availability" of such a memory can be influenced by how much time has passed, or whether the event was unusual for some reason and, in turn, can influence judgment. In order to safeguard against availability bias, interviewers provide participants with documents and

[1] This subsection is based on the presentation by M. Granger Morgan, Professor and Head of the Department of Engineering and Public Policy, Carnegie Mellon University.

visual aids to ensure that they have the full complement of information in mind when answering questions.

Anchoring and Adjustment

If people start with a first value ("anchor") and then adjust up and down from that value, they typically do not adjust sufficiently. It is best not to begin an elicitation with a question about what is the "best" or "most probable" value, but rather to begin work by establishing outer ranges and then move in toward estimates of best value, said Morgan.

Bayesian Approaches[2]

Joel Greenhouse, Professor of Statistics, Carnegie Mellon University, described how Bayesian approaches can permit the introduction of judgments about plausible values within a given study to be taken into account in forming conclusions about the treatment effect being studied. By incorporating consideration of how an RCT changes our opinion about a treatment effect, Bayesian statistical approaches could help the scientific and regulatory communities come to agreement about the treatment effect seen in a clinical trial, noted Greenhouse.

To set the stage and provide a common terminology, Greenhouse explained that conventional statistical analysis calculates a single probability value (p-value) for its hypothesis in a clinical trial—either that one treatment represents a gain over another, or that it has no effect at all. Before an RCT begins, the Bayesian approach instead calculates a probability distribution of the plausible values of the treatment effect. This probability distribution excludes evidence from the current RCT and forms the "prior distribution." Then, based on emerging information from the current RCT, a plausible value of the treatment effect is generated, or "likelihood." Applying Bayes rule and Bayesian methodology, the prior distribution is combined with the likelihood to determine the "posterior distribution" that is ultimately a combination of historical assessments of a treatment effect and current opinion about the treatment effect in the active RCT.

Greenhouse noted that the prior distribution can also be adjusted to take into account judgments about whether particular information should be discounted. For example, previous studies believed to be relevant, but

---

[2] This subsection is based on the presentation by Joel Greenhouse, Professor of Statistics, Carnegie Mellon University, and material from *Characterizing Uncertainty in the Assessment of Benefits and Risks of Pharmaceutical Products: Workshop in Brief* (IOM, 2014), also prepared for this project.

not directly related, might be "downweighted," which has the effect of reducing the sample size of that relevant prior information. The likelihood and prior distribution are ways to formalize and make transparent assumptions by representing uncertainties in terms of probability distributions. The posterior distribution then summarizes the belief about the treatment effect. Greenhouse added that sensitivity analysis can be used to test how assumptions about the prior distribution affect the posterior inference. He noted that "[i]f it does not change very much, that gives you added confidence that the conclusions are not being driven by the prior [distribution]. If it does change a lot, that . . . tells you how much uncertainty you have . . . in the available evidence about the question of interest."

Key to the Bayesian approach is summarizing and synthesizing evidence that can inform the specifications of these probability distributions. With this in mind, Greenhouse posed the question, "What is the role for non-RCT sources of evidence to help inform the FDA about questions of effectiveness and safety?"

Over the course of the workshops, several participants cited the promise of Bayesian approaches to evaluating clinical trial data and the potential for more robust characterization of inferences drawn from studies. Application of a disciplined Bayesian approach could offer opportunities to characterize and accommodate uncertainty in clinical trials.

APPLYING DECISION THEORY APPROACHES TO REGULATORY DECISION MAKING

Several speaker presentations generally addressed decision theory *techniques* and the *scientific basis for incorporating patient and other stakeholder preferences*. Several speakers suggested that scientific methodologies for the incorporation of expert deliberation and stakeholder perspectives can help to improve certainty of forecasts, place what is known and what is unknown in a practical context, address uncertainties in the context of patient preferences, reveal new uncertainties that otherwise might have been overlooked, and provide important information on values for regulatory determinations.

Lessons from the Intelligence Community[3]

David R. Mandel, Senior Scientist, Socio-Cognitive Systems, Defence Research and Development Canada (DRDC), Toronto Research Centre,

[3] This subsection is based on the presentation by David R. Mandel, Senior Scientist, Socio-Cognitive Systems, Defence Research and Development Canada (DRDC), Toronto Research Centre.

provided a perspective on characterizing uncertainty from the domain of intelligence assessments. Mandel noted that he is currently working on a 3-year study to assess the ability of clinical researchers to accurately predict both operational and scientific outcomes of RCTs.

Mandel reinforced Morgan's comments that language is severely limited in its ability to convey accurate information, noting that "words are imprecise and vague, their imprecision varies across individuals, and is not necessarily aligned with normative meanings."

One conventional corrective measure, he noted, is the prohibition of "weasel words" and phrases, such as "reportedly," "evidence suggests (or indicates)," "distinctly possible," and "apparently." According to Mandel, this language seems to insinuate more than the analyst is willing to commit or likely to be held accountable for. If the prediction turns out to be wrong, the analyst can then "weasel" out of responsibility. Another corrective approach is to institutionalize a rank ordering of verbal probability using specific and common definitions. However, Mandel noted, such approaches do little to reduce the vagueness associated with the selected terms and there is no guarantee that decision makers will keep the prescribed rank ordering in mind when reading reports.

A more radical proposal, he said, would be to assign numbers to words that communicate uncertainty (see Figure 4-1 for two examples of verbal probability terms). When standards are applied consistently, numbers can "smoke out the weasels," he noted. Numbers also can be operated on, whereas the equation "[likely (times) very improbable]" cannot be solved. In addition, numbers can clearly communicate imprecision; for example, an analyst can be 95 percent confident that the probability of an event is 70 percent, plus or minus 10 percent. Even if numbers are only used internally, such as for audit purposes, they lend themselves to verification of judgment quality, detection of systematic biases, and subsequent correction.

No matter what method is selected to clarify the meanings of uncertainty words, Mandel said, a critical issue is to make clear to the reader what is certain knowledge and what is reasoned judgment, including a way to communicate the degree of certitude that supports each key statement.

Stakeholder Elicitation Methods[4]

Joseph Arvai, Professor and Svare Chair in Applied Decision Research, Department of Geography, Institute for Sustainable Energy, Environment,

[4] This subsection is based on the presentation by Joseph Arvai, Professor and Svare Chair in Applied Decision Research, Department of Geography, Institute for Sustainable Energy, Environment, and Economy, University of Calgary.

Impact						
	Severe 5	Significant	High	High	Very High	Very High
	Major 4	Medium	Significant	High	High	High
	Moderate 3	Low	Medium	Significant	Significant	High
	Minor 2	Low	Low	Medium	Medium	Significant
	Insignificant 1	Low	Low	Low	Medium	Medium
		Rare 1	Unlikely 2	Possible 3	Likely 4	Almost Certain 5
		Likelihood				

Risk Assessment Matrix						
		Probability				
Severity		Frequent A	Likely B	Occasional C	Seldom D	Unlikely E
Catastrophic	I	E	E	H	H	M
Critical	II	E	H	H	M	L
Marginal	III	H	M	M	L	L
Negligible	IV	M	L	L	L	L

FIGURE 4-1 Example of inconsistent use of verbal probability terms from two standards produced by the same government department.
KEY: E = Extremely High; H = High; L = Low; M = Medium.
SOURCE: Adapted from Mandel, 2007.

and Economy, University of Calgary, stated that decision theory provides a structured approach for gauging the influence of individual perspectives, including a scientific rationale for incorporating stakeholder input in benefit–risk considerations.

Decision research often works with *preferences*, which represent an individual's attitude toward a set of alternatives. Preferences are not static beliefs to be uncovered, as an archaeologist might seek an object; instead, Arvai said, preferences are *constructed* at three key points during the decision process: (1) when the decision is identified as complex or novel; (2) when translation between data and values is necessary to make the decision; and (3) when trade-offs must be made between alternatives and objectives.

When these trade-offs between alternatives and objectives will affect many stakeholders, eliciting their input is effective in helping individuals understand the choices available to them; this enhanced understanding might in turn shape the preferences of decision makers.

Arvai cited his work on point-of-use water treatment options in East Africa as having similar traits to a doctor–patient discussion about treatment options. The community's question about their water supply was, "What treatment for our water supply will work best both in terms of keeping us healthy and aligning with our cultural values?" To answer this question, Arvai's team compiled information about the sources of water that people were using and the treatment options that were available. They then met with the relevant stakeholders to present the options, and which ones might best serve their needs.

After some hands-on experience with each of the treatments, the members of the community scored them according to which ones best satisfied their objectives. The results concluded that the most desirable treatment for the villagers was not the one that was being distributed by the aid agencies.

The same type of process, Arvai said, could be used in the context of treatment choices between a doctor and a patient, or between a regulator and a drug maker. A stakeholder elicitation process could produce a list of objectives and performance measures for treatments, ranked against the range of alternatives available. This would allow participants to test-run different scenarios and decide which alternative best meets their objectives.

Such approaches are not new. Arvai cited publications (see Appendix C for additional resources) that explicate several methods by which structured, deliberative processes can combine stakeholder input with analysis. Although structured decision making does not always deal explicitly with uncertainty, Arvai noted that in addition to sensitivity analysis, composite indexes have been developed to assess uncertainty across a suite of attributes. In this process, he said, "tolerance for uncertainty" can be treated as its own objective and included in the assessment of alternatives.

Eliciting Values for Risk Management[5]

Timothy McDaniels, Professor, Faculty of Science, Institute of Resources and Environment, University of British Columbia, stated that eliciting values for risk management choices is a process of applying *structured common sense* to complex problems. This includes a reliance on the concept of what is known as decision making under "deep uncertainty," a condition that exists when the parties to a decision do not know, or do not agree on, the system models that relate actions to consequences. The concept of decision making under deep certainty about the future provides one basis and rationale for statistical decision theory.

Key to eliciting values for risk management is the consideration of *alternatives*, said McDaniels. Well-managed regulatory approval decisions consider the available alternatives to the proposed drug and the consequences of not approving it. The central valuation question that drives a risk management process, said McDaniels, is this:

> Given the estimated impacts of the alternatives on these objectives, *is it worthwhile for society to accept the trade-offs in going from "do not approve" to "approve" for one of the alternatives?*

McDaniels offered several concepts about the importance of including alternatives in risk decisions:

- The acceptable level of risk for a given decision should be a function of the available alternatives, *not a single scientific threshold*. Although thresholds can simplify, they also mask trade-offs or disregard them altogether.
- Managing a decision process in order to *improve alternatives*, or to build in less undesirable alternatives, is one approach to achieving better risk management outcomes.
- When faced with deep uncertainties, learning over time and flexibility to adapt to different contexts are key components of the process that could promote the consideration of robust and resilient alternatives over a wide range of uncertainties.
- Decisions must be made before all uncertainties are resolved; therefore, "surprises" are a potential part of any risk management process.

He discussed several components to the valuation process for managing risk, using the Tysabri case study to note those that he found FDA had

[5] This subsection is based on the presentation by Timothy McDaniels, Professor, Faculty of Science, Institute of Resources and Environment, University of British Columbia.

already adopted successfully. The ideal process, he said, is a legitimate, transparent management process that supports making informed choices among alternatives within an insightful, well-structured framework. This includes both technical (scientific) information and value-based information (preferences) to clarify and examine trade-offs, which should be addressed explicitly and distinctly. In this regard, said McDaniels, FDA is in an enviable position relative to many risk governance bodies. FDA has clear authority, domain expertise, respect, abundant data, flexibility, and the capacity to monitor.

Also, values are context dependent; thus, eliciting values for risk choices can be most effective when focused on a specific regulatory decision process, as does FDA's benefit–risk framework. In addition, noted McDaniels, FDA makes good use of its advisory committee structure as a forum for combining analysis and reflection on values.

FDA APPROACHES TO DECISION MAKING

In addition to McDaniels' previous comments on FDA's decision processes, individual workshop participants also noted a number of FDA attributes and processes that currently incorporate, or could be enhanced to incorporate, the methods and approaches of decision science for making decisions under uncertainty.

FDA Authority and Processes

McDaniels commented that FDA has clear authority conferred on it by statute, with transparent processes allowing for an environment in which informed choices can be made among alternatives within a structured framework. He further noted that FDA has adopted an approach for eliciting stakeholder values through the consultative process the agency is employing in developing its benefit–risk framework. Several workshop participants, including Lisa LaVange, Director, Office of Biostatistics, Office of Translational Sciences, CDER, FDA, noted that FDA has established processes and mechanisms for engaging experts in regulatory decision making, most notably through the convening of advisory committees. McDaniels noted that the advisory panel structure could potentially be further enhanced through a structured or formal attention to stakeholder values elicited through that process.

Bayesian Statistical Methods

Formal Bayesian methods have not been adopted generally by FDA for the evaluation of pharmaceuticals. According to LaVange, however, there are several possible applications for Bayesian methods to be considered, including safety studies, where evidence accumulates over time; non-inferiority trials, because they call for the incorporation of historical data of one or more comparator drug(s); and antibiotics development, in part because the mechanism of action is more evident: "I can look at a dish of bugs and see if a drug kills them."

Risk Evaluation and Mitigation Strategy Mechanism

Several workshop participants, including Theresa Mullin, FDA, noted that the Food and Drug Administration Amendments Act of 2007 gave FDA the authority to require a REMS in connection with approval of a marketing application (or later if new safety information emerges). FDA might require a REMS if it determines such action necessary to ensure that the benefits of a drug or biological product outweigh its risks. As outlined in FDA's Draft REMS Guidance for Industry (FDA, 2009a), REMS could include, as required by FDA, a special medication guide or patient package insert; a communication plan targeted to health care providers; and elements to ensure safe use, including patient registration, physician training, certification, or other monitoring. McDaniels commented that to the extent that the REMS structure provides more approval alternatives (other than approve without conditions/disapprove) and includes ability to learn over time from monitoring, such a system constitutes a valuable tool for applying risk-management choices in a structured format.

Proposed New Regulatory Pathways

Individual workshop participants raised questions about new regulatory approval pathways that could address certain aspects of uncertainty in the drug review process. For example, Special Medical Use (SMU) is a proposed limited-use approval pathway for drugs developed in an expedited manner to meet unmet medical needs in a clearly defined subpopulation. One workshop participant noted that the pathway was proposed in part to take into account that certain severely affected subpopulations with few treatment options might be willing to accept greater uncertainty and greater risk. The SMU regulatory mechanism would limit use of products approved under that pathway to specified populations while requiring additional evidence development and safety surveillance in the postmarket setting prior to the product receiving an unrestricted approval for use in broader populations.

Charles F. Manski, Board of Trustees Professor in Economics, Northwestern University, discussed the role of identification problems in evaluating uncertainty for drug reviews, and the potential for "adaptive approval" licensing approaches to mitigate them. In econometrics, examining the quality of inferences made from empirical evidence can address one of two components, identification and statistics.

According to Manski, it is an identification problem when evidence wrongly identifies a relationship between a treatment effect and a health outcome. For instance, many issues with trials, such as issues with statistical design, research participant adherence and retention, and extrapolating outcomes from surrogates, could lead to identification problems. It is the dominant source of error in drug approval, he said, and identification problems would persist even if statistical imprecision were eliminated.

Manski indicated that all drug approvals are made with limited data; while unavoidable, this makes regulatory decisions susceptible to two types of errors. Type I, the "false positive" error that occurs when approved drugs are ineffective or unsafe, might eventually be corrected through additional research (assuming the drug gets to market). However, Manski noted, Type II, the "false negative" error of a worthy drug failing approval, could be permanent if the drug is pulled from development and no further data are produced.

Manski suggested broadening the set of approval options beyond yes or no, by empowering FDA to institute what he termed *adaptive partial approval*, similar in concept to "adaptive licensing" proposals made by others in the field (Eichler et al., 2012). The adaptive mechanism suggested by Manski could allow for earlier approval of a broader class of products than those contemplated in the SMU proposal, he said, coupled with limited use and further evidence-gathering requirements. Limited-term and limited-quantity sales licenses could be granted while Phase III trials are under way, and the duration of Phase III trials could be longer than they typically are at present, enabling measurement of real, rather than surrogate, outcomes. He noted that in this way FDA could make decisions based on outcomes data.

A related idea, Manski added, would be to design *response-adaptive trials* that sequentially draw participants into traditional RCTs, then allocate new participants based on the health outcomes observed in earlier participants. The objective is to "use the observed response data to adapt the allocation probabilities, so that more patients will hopefully receive the better treatment" (Tamura et al., 1994, p. 768). Manski acknowledged that adaptive partial approval would require a systemic change in drug regulation, raising many issues, including the impact on innovation. Workshop participants also noted that retention of participants in ongoing clinical trials could be undermined by the availability on the market, even on a limited basis, of the product being studied.

5

Communicating Uncertainty

Key Messages Identified by Individual Speakers

- Effective risk communication can help people make informed decisions by providing structured ways to understand the uncertainties inherent in the choices with which they are presented.
- FDA press releases are often the source of primary information for the media and can be a tool for conveying benefit, harm, and uncertainty information to the public.
- Implementing standard procedures for developing and communicating regulatory decisions could improve the accuracy and impact of risk communication strategies.
- Public information at the time of a drug's approval can be improved by clearly conveying benefits, harms, and uncertainties and concisely highlighting what is known, what is still being studied, and what is unknown.
- FDA uses a number of tools to communicate benefits, risks, and uncertainties to a variety of audiences.

Treating uncertainty in a structured manner can produce better and more useful science. Baruch Fischhoff, Carnegie Mellon University, explained that better science results from disciplined reflection on the uncertainties inherent in evidence, and useful science is the result of taking the needs of the decision maker into account. Crafting messages to communicate the outcomes of science, and the inherent uncertainties, presents a powerful opportunity to inform and improve the decisions made by individuals. A number of workshop participants indicated that communicating uncertainty is at the heart of many of the issues and challenges associated with benefit–risk assessments.

OVERVIEW OF RISK COMMUNICATION[1]

The intent of effective risk communication is to help people make informed decisions; it does so by providing orderly, structured ways to understand the uncertainties inherent in their choices, explained Fischhoff. To make those informed choices, individuals need to understand both the facts and their own values: What positive and negative outcomes might follow each possible choice? Which set of possible outcomes offers the most acceptable trade-offs?

Individuals do not always realize that both facts and values can involve uncertainty, said Fischhoff. As an example of uncertainty about facts, for reasons that are unknown, a drug might produce the expected outcome for one person and not for another. Uncertainties about facts arise from three inevitable aspects of scientific research: (1) imperfections in evidence (internal validity), (2) differences between evidence and actual experience (external validity), and (3) the possibility of surprises in the underlying science. As examples of uncertainties about values, people might be so unfamiliar with some of the effects of a drug that they cannot predict their reactions to it or they might have erroneous expectations about their responses.

The job of a communicator is to find out which uncertainties are important to the individual, and deliver scientifically grounded messages that provide that information. Fischhoff indicated that poor communication about uncertainty can cause:

- *Needless hesitation*. People might postpone a decision while trying to get more information, when the uncertainty actually lies in their preferences.
- *Unwarranted confidence*. People might think they know themselves and their circumstance better than is actually the case.
- *Inappropriate choices*. People would have made better choices if they had a better understanding of the uncertainties.

[1] This section is based on the presentation by Baruch Fischhoff, Howard Heinz University Professor, Department of Social and Decision Sciences, Department of Engineering and Public Policy, Carnegie Mellon University.

- *Personal regret.* People wish that they had made a different choice, which would have been possible with better understanding of the uncertainties.
- *Interpersonal resentment.* People might blame others who, they believe, should have helped them work through these uncertainties.

As the literature of risk communication demonstrates, Fischhoff noted, scientific rigor is needed to create accurate messages. Underlying any risk communication is an implicit decision tree representing the choice that the communicator seeks to inform (see Figure 5-1). Making that tree explicit allows a disciplined approach to selecting relevant information.

Fischhoff explained that there are three concerns of experts that can hamper taking a scientific approach to communicating uncertainty. First, experts might be reluctant to express uncertainty, which they perceive as misplaced imprecision. The second is that experts might have such a poor opinion of lay audiences that they expect to be misunderstood. The third is that experts might be afraid of being punished, by their employers or colleagues, for being candid about uncertainties.

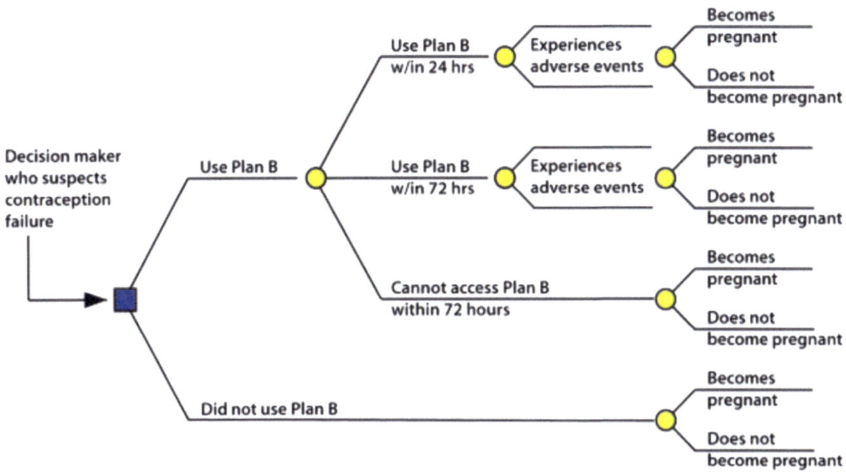

FIGURE 5-1 Decision tree for Plan B use after suspected contraceptive failure. Decision trees represent decision options, outcomes, and their associated uncertainties.

SOURCE: Reprinted from *Social Science & Medicine,* 67(4), T. Krishnamurti, S. L. Eggers, and B. Fischhoff, The impact of over-the-counter availability of "Plan B" on teens' contraceptive decision making, 67:618-627, 2008, with permission from Elsevier.

Fischhoff offered two proposals to regulatory decision makers that could improve their risk communication efforts:

1. *Create standard procedures for making and communicating decisions.* FDA's benefit–risk framework (see Figure 1-1) provides a sound structure for summarizing uncertainty. Fischhoff noted the Prescription Drug Facts Box as a means for communicating that summary (see Figure 5-3).
2. *Create a resource center for eliciting and communicating uncertainty.* Fischhoff noted that current support for risk communication efforts is largely haphazard and episodic. Establishing dedicated resource centers, akin to the statistics units (or "cores") that are part of large medical research projects, would allow medical experts to receive high-quality support for applying the science of communication to conveying their science and its uncertainties. Such a center would provide:

    - Quality assurance for eliciting and communicating uncertainty;
    - Economies of scope, by addressing recurrent issues with a common base of knowledge;
    - Enhanced professional relationships between scientists and communications, built on trust and mutual respect; and
    - Stimulus for basic applied research, addressing communication challenges emerging from the work.

INCREASING PUBLIC AWARENESS AND UNDERSTANDING OF UNCERTAINTY

Decision Making from the Patient's Perspective[2]

Regulators routinely evaluate a drug's benefits and risks for a population, and health care providers routinely evaluate those benefits and risks for their individual patients. But the patients must ultimately weigh all of the information available to them in the context of their unique values, needs, and expectations, said Kimberly McCleary, Director, Strategic Initiatives, *FasterCures*.[3]

Patients are looking to answer three questions, she said: What benefits am I trying to enhance with the treatment I am considering, what

[2] This subsection is based on the presentation by Kimberly McCleary, Director, Strategic Initiatives, *FasterCures*.

[3] For more information on *FasterCures*' Benefit–Risk Assessment program, see http://www.fastercures.org/r-and-d-policy/benefit-risk-assessment (accessed September 12, 2014).

risks or harms am I trying to avoid or mitigate, and how confident am I about the information I have at hand to make these decisions? Patients must contend with myriad inputs and influences that complicate their choices, and the choices themselves may change with time and changing circumstances.

To illustrate the complexity of the patient decision-making process, McCleary provided an overview of the sources of information and influence that affect uncertainty about treatment options. They include

- **Purpose of the treatment option**
  - Is it for disease prevention, or is it curative? For a chronic condition, or to delay a chronic condition from developing? Acute care for life saving, or palliative care for end of life?
- **Treatment options**
  - Medication, surgery, in-hospital treatments, cognitive therapy, "nutraceuticals," possible inclusion in clinical trial
- **Family decisions and family attitudes**
- **Information sources**
  - Peers, co-workers, friends
  - The Internet (ranging from well informed, seemingly well informed, and not even pretending to be well informed)
  - Support groups for various conditions, and these can be very well-organized, professionally facilitated support groups that have a particular intention in terms of informing about the choices
  - Loosely organized online discussion groups
  - Media coverage
- **Other factors**
  - Insurance coverage, reimbursement, out-of-pocket costs, disability vs. employment, geographic proximity to treatment location, and support system

McCleary noted that to date, there has been no structured process for patients to evaluate all these factors in the context of their own personal and medical situations.[4] Instead, as is true for anyone making decisions, people will make their choices based on whatever information is accessible, most memorable, or best fits with their values.

[4] For an example of a patient-focused, structured decision-making approach, see the presentation in Chapter 3 by Robyn Lim, Senior Science Advisor, Office of Legislative and Regulatory Modernization, Health Products and Food Branch, Health Canada, on Health Canada's Benefit–Harm–Uncertainty Initiative.

Communicating Uncertainty About Benefits and Harms of Pharmaceuticals[5]

Four common uncertainties are present at the time of approval that affect most, if not all, drugs, according to Lisa M. Schwartz, Professor, Departments of Medicine and Community & Family Medicine, Dartmouth Medical School; and Co-Director, Center for Medicine and the Media, at The Dartmouth Institute for Health Policy and Clinical Practice, and Steven Woloshin, Professor, Departments of Medicine and Community & Family Medicine, Dartmouth Medical School; and Co-Director, Center for Medicine and the Media, at The Dartmouth Institute for Health Policy and Clinical Practice.

1. *Standard uncertainty.* According to Woloshin, the standard uncertainty that applies to all new drugs has to do with their limited track record. To get drugs to market in a reasonable amount of time, approvals generally are based on relatively short-term clinical studies involving limited numbers of patients. Furthermore, clinical trials for regulatory approval are designed to detect benefit, not harm. Consequently, it cannot be known at the time of approval how well a drug's benefits or safety will hold up over time when a drug is taken over periods of time that are longer than the trial duration. Unfortunately, Woloshin said, it is not unusual for serious adverse effects to emerge after large numbers of people use a drug for long periods of time.

While clinicians and researchers are usually aware that the true effects of new drugs are inherently uncertain, patients might not understand. This leads to what Woloshin called the standard misconception that "new is better." This misconception is reinforced in advertisements targeting physicians and consumers that promote a drug's newness as representing extra benefit, rather than extra uncertainty, noted Woloshin.

In an attempt to offset this misconception, regulators in Europe and the United Kingdom require companies to include a "black triangle" warning next to the name of a new drug on all prescriber and consumer information, alongside the statement "This medicinal product is subject to additional monitoring."[6] The intent is to alert the public that despite a rigorous approval process, the drug is "under probation," as Woloshin

[5] This subsection is based on the presentation by Lisa M. Schwartz, Professor, Departments of Medicine and Community & Family Medicine, Dartmouth Medical School; and Co-Director, Center for Medicine and the Media, at The Dartmouth Institute for Health Policy and Clinical Practice, and Steven Woloshin, Professor, Departments of Medicine and Community & Family Medicine, Dartmouth Medical School; and Co-Director, Center for Medicine and the Media, at The Dartmouth Institute for Health Policy and Clinical Practice.

[6] For more information on the European Union's use of the "black triangle" scheme, see http://www.mhra.gov.uk/Safetyinformation/Howwemonitorthesafetyofproducts/Medicines/BlackTriangleproducts/index.htm (accessed September 12, 2014).

termed it, reminding consumers that a drug's track record is established over time as greater numbers of people use it over a longer period of time.

To test how communicating the concepts inherent in the black triangle would affect consumer enthusiasm for new drugs in the United States, Schwartz and Woloshin conducted a national randomized trial of approximately 3,000 adults (Schwartz and Woloshin, 2011). Participants were asked to choose between two heartburn drugs with the same benefits and harms—with the only difference being that one drug was approved in the current year and the other had been approved 8 years earlier. The control group received no other information, but the intervention group was told, "As with all new drugs, rare but serious drug side effects may emerge after the drug is on the market—when larger numbers of people have used the drug." Woloshin reported that the study found that the simple one-sentence warning dampened enthusiasm for the new drug. The warning reduced the proportion of patients choosing the new drug by 19 percent (66 percent vs. 47 percent, 95 percent confidence interval: 13 to 24 percent) (Schwartz and Woloshin, 2011).

Woloshin suggested that graphics like the black triangle or text-only warnings should be applied to new drugs for the first few years they are on the market to highlight this inherent uncertainty to the public. He noted that the IOM study (2007) also called for the implementation of this new drug warning on all product labels.

2. *Extra uncertainty due to accelerated approval.* The second common uncertainty results when there is limited evidence of benefit at the time of approval. For example, drugs that are subject to FDA's accelerated approval process when they are intended to treat serious diseases with limited treatment options. This approval pathway permits drawing on preliminary evidence (e.g., trials might use a surrogate endpoint as the primary outcome, might employ a single-arm design, or might be shorter in duration than FDA's standard) to speed new drugs to patients who need them. A total of 11.7 percent (22 out of 188) of novel therapeutic agents approved by FDA between 2005 and 2012 were reviewed through the accelerated approval mechanism (Downing et al., 2014).

Woloshin explained that while the concept of accelerated approval is very useful and important, information conveying that there is extra uncertainty due to the accelerated nature of the approval is often buried in the various communication tools deployed by FDA. He argued that this uncertainty should be highlighted and featured prominently for physicians and patients. To illustrate, Woloshin compared the information on the package insert for Tysabri, a product that received accelerated approval, to what he considered a more appropriate disclosure (see Figures 5-2 and 5-3). Recent FDA guidance to industry on drug labeling

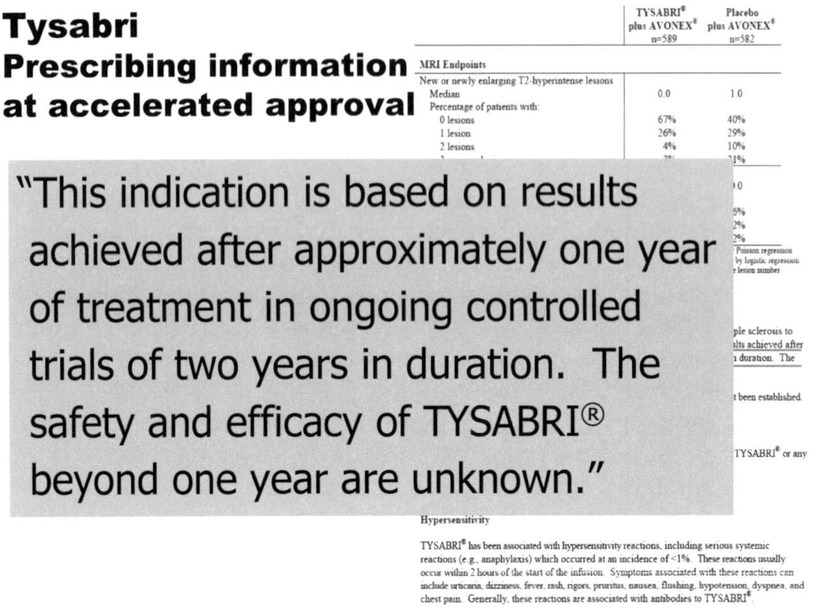

FIGURE 5-2 Tysabri prescribing information appearing on page 4 of the package insert.
SOURCE: Schwartz and Woloshin, 2014. Presentation at the IOM workshop series on Characterizing and Communicating Uncertainty in the Assessment of Benefits and Risks of Pharmaceutical Products.

now calls for this type of disclosure in the "Highlights" section of a drug label (FDA, 2014).

3. *Extra uncertainty based on surrogate primary outcomes*. Approximately half (48.9 percent) of the pivotal clinical trials for novel therapeutic agents approved by FDA between 2005 and 2012 included a surrogate outcome as the primary endpoint (Downing et al., 2014).[7] Surrogates should translate into patient outcomes, said Schwartz, but they do not always. For example, the drug Iressa was approved to treat advanced lung cancer on the basis of the surrogate outcome of tumor shrinkage seen on X-rays. The hope was that tumor shrinkage would translate into reduction of lung cancer deaths. Unfortunately in this case, when the required randomized trial was completed, Iressa did not reduce lung cancer death and the drug's label was changed to limit use in certain cancer patients.

[7] A surrogate outcome is intended to substitute for a clinical endpoint; for example, lower blood pressure might serve as a surrogate for lower rates of heart disease.

Tysabri (natalizumab) monotherapy for relapsing multiple sclerosis

Study Findings

942 people with relapsing multiple sclerosis who had at least 1 relapse in the past year were randomized to TYSABRI or PLACEBO for 2 years. Here's what happened at the end of **1 year**:

	TYSABRI (300mg IV every 4 weeks)	**PLACEBO**
How did Tysabri help?		
Percent of people with no relapses (23% more had no relapses)	76%	53%
Change in disability	Unknown	

Bottom line

- **Accelerated approval based on the 1-year results of a planned 2-year trial** Because other multiple sclerosis drugs were all approved based on 2-year results, Tysabri's approval is conditional on the results holding up at 2 years.

"The clinical meaningfulness of a decrease in the relapse rate through only one year is uncertain...The effect at 1 year can be considered as a surrogate for an effect at 2 years. The usual limitations of a surrogate must be borne in mind, in particular the difficulty in reliably predicting the magnitude of natalizumab's effect at 2 years." FDA Medical Reviewer

FIGURE 5-3 A Tysabri Drug Facts Box suggested by Woloshin and Schwartz to concisely highlight what was known, still being studied, and unknown at the time of Tysabri's accelerated approval.
SOURCE: Schwartz and Woloshin, 2014. Presentation at the IOM workshop series on Characterizing and Communicating Uncertainty in the Assessment of Benefits and Risks of Pharmaceutical Products.

Because of the fundamental uncertainty of surrogate outcomes, Schwartz said, it is important that patients understand the inherent uncertainty when drug approvals are based on surrogate outcomes. The same randomized trial mentioned above (Schwartz and Woloshin, 2011) tested people's perspectives on the concepts behind surrogate outcomes. The results revealed that a simple, 23-word, non-directive explanation about surrogate outcomes resulted in 12 percent more people (71 percent vs. 59 percent, 95 percent confidence interval: 7 to 18 percent) correctly choosing a drug that reduced myocardial infarctions over one only known to improve cholesterol levels.

Educating patients about the uncertainties of drugs approved on the basis of a surrogate outcome matters, Schwartz explained, because such drugs might be heavily promoted through direct-to-consumer advertising. For example, Zetia was heavily advertised to the public for several years before FDA began requiring that the prescribing information and marketing materials include the statement, "The effect of Zetia on cardiovascular morbidity and mortality has not been determined." Schwartz indicated that this statement is an important step in the right direction, but FDA should also ensure that these crucial messages about uncertainty are routinely communicated to patients and are not buried at the bottom of lengthy, dense documents.

4. *Extra uncertainty based on signals of harm.* Schwartz suggested that when data supporting a newly approved drug indicate a potential signal of harm strong enough for FDA to require postmarketing studies, this is an important signal of uncertainty that should be clearly shared with patients. Many drugs are aggressively promoted, potentially increasing patient misunderstanding regarding the fundamental uncertainties about benefits and harms still being evaluated. Schwartz indicated that FDA could improve the consistency and impact of its communications by prominently featuring information about postmarketing requirements in press releases, information for prescribers, and labeling. Schwartz also noted the importance of including information about the direction of the uncertainty—for example, if the uncertainty is not that the effect of a drug on an outcome is unknown, but that there is an open question about a potential harm and that FDA is requiring specific postmarketing studies to better understand the magnitude of the problem. Box 5-1 includes a summary of routine disclosures for regulators suggested by Schwartz and Woloshin to proactively communicate uncertainties about newly approved drugs to the public.

The Drug Facts Box

Schwartz suggested that information about uncertainty is most helpful in the context of what is known about a drug's benefits and harms. In general, people are more likely to tolerate uncertainties when the benefit-to-harm ratio is large than when it is small. Schwartz and Woloshin suggest that FDA consider summarizing the facts about benefits, harms, and uncertainties in a reader-friendly format such as the Drug Facts Box, a one-page summary of benefit and harm data for each indication of a drug that includes explicit acknowledgment of uncertainties (Schwartz and Woloshin, 2013). Schwartz noted that members of FDA's Risk Communication Advisory Committee unanimously voted that FDA should adopt the Drug Facts Box as its standard format (FDA, 2009b), and the Affordable Care Act[8] also suggests that FDA conduct a pilot study of the Drug Facts Box to improve communication.

[8] Patient Protection and Affordable Care Act of 2012. Pub. L. No. 111-148, § 3507, 124 Stat. 119, 530 (codified at note following 21 U.S.C. § 352).

BOX 5-1[a]
Suggested Routine Disclosures for Regulators

Based on the common uncertainties that are present at the time any new drug is approved, Schwartz and Woloshin recommended a proactive approach to communicating these uncertainties to the public.

Flag New Drugs for the First Few Years on the Market
Use a graphic or text to communicate that the limited experience with new drugs means greater uncertainty.

Warn When Evidence of Benefit Is Especially Weak
Be clear about the extra uncertainty inherent with study duration shorter than FDA standard or use of surrogate outcome measures.

Point Out Postmarketing Trials Required for Signals of Harm
Specify what postmarketing trials were required, why, and when results will be available—in the Highlights of the label (in either "Limitations of Use" or "Warnings & Precautions" sections).

Prominently Acknowledge Uncertainty at Approval
Explain uncertainties about benefit or harm in FDA press releases, the professional label, and consumer information.

[a] This box is based on the presentation by Lisa M. Schwartz, Professor, Departments of Medicine and Community & Family Medicine, Dartmouth Medical School; and Co-Director, Center for Medicine and the Media, at The Dartmouth Institute for Health Policy and Clinical Practice, and Steven Woloshin, Professor, Departments of Medicine and Community & Family Medicine, Dartmouth Medical School; and Co-Director, Center for Medicine and the Media, at The Dartmouth Institute for Health Policy and Clinical Practice.

COMMUNICATING UNCERTAINTY: FDA AND MEDIA MESSAGES ABOUT TYSABRI[9]

Tysabri (natalizumab) was approved by FDA in 2004, on an accelerated schedule, as a promising new drug to treat patients with relapsing MS. Four months later, it was withdrawn from the market after two people developed a rare, deadly brain infection called PML. The drug

[9] This section is based on the presentation by Lisa M. Schwartz, Professor, Departments of Medicine and Community & Family Medicine, Dartmouth Medical School; and Co-Director, Center for Medicine and the Media, at The Dartmouth Institute for Health Policy and Clinical Practice, and Steven Woloshin, Professor, Departments of Medicine and Community & Family Medicine, Dartmouth Medical School; and Co-Director, Center for Medicine and the Media, at The Dartmouth Institute for Health Policy and Clinical Practice.

was reintroduced after risk factors for PML were identified (see Box 3-3 for details about Tysabri).

Schwartz and Woloshin presented an analysis of media reports about Tysabri, focusing on the presentation of benefits, harms, and uncertainties stemming from the accelerated approval process, and the risk of PML. The analysis included 76 stories from major newspapers, and national radio and television transcripts for the 2 months following each of six major milestones in the story of Tysabri. The six milestones selected were: (1) Tysabri approval in 2004, (2) Tysabri withdrawal in 2005 after identification of two PML cases, (3) the convening of a 2006 FDA advisory committee meeting on Tysabri, (4) the remarketing approval of Tysabri in 2006, (5) the 2008 emergence of the first two new cases of PML after remarketing, and (6) FDA's 2012 announcement of the first test to help determine the risk of PML in people taking Tysabri. Schwartz and Woloshin cautioned that the results they presented were preliminary.

FDA Messaging About Tysabri

Woloshin provided an excerpt from the FDA press release (2004) at the time of Tysabri's original approval:

> This innovative treatment for multiple sclerosis represents a new approach to treating MS—exciting news for patients with this serious disease. . . . While we eagerly await long-term results from ongoing clinical trials, we have reason to believe that Tysabri will significantly reduce relapses in MS.

Woloshin characterized this statement on the first page of the press release as overly enthusiastic, noting that the statement exhibited the standard misconception that new is better. The press release also failed to highlight the uncertainty that is inherent to all new drugs, and the extra uncertainty that existed because Tysabri received accelerated approval.

Also in the initial FDA press release was a statement that the approval of Tysabri was based on positive results seen in patients after 1 year of treatment:

> The approval of Tysabri is based on positive results seen in patients after one year of treatment. This product received accelerated approval because it appears to provide substantial benefit for patients with a serious disease. As part of that approval, the manufacturer has committed to continuing its trials of this product for another year.

The reason presented for accelerated approval is factually correct, said Woloshin. The press release clearly acknowledges that long-term results are pending and that approval was based on 1 year of clinical trial data instead of 2 years. However, he said, the press release did not state that all previous MS drugs were approved on 2 years of evidence, that the Tysabri approval was a departure from the norm, and that the shorter track record increased uncertainty about outcomes.

Also, Woloshin noted, the release included no acknowledgment that Tysabri's effect on disability progression—another important clinical outcome—was unknown at the time of approval, but which the company was required to report when 2-year study data were available. The FDA press release also quantified the effect of the drug with a relative risk reduction (i.e., Tysabri reduced the frequency of relapses by 66 percent relative to placebo). But stating relative changes without also stating the base rate can exaggerate the perceived benefit of an intervention. For instance, imagine hearing that items in a store are 30 percent off without knowing what they cost originally. Woloshin explained that using the term "30 percent off" means much more savings with expensive items compared to less expensive ones. Woloshin further suggested that a clearer message about the effect of Tysabri would have been to indicate that, compared to a placebo, the drug reduced the relapse rate from 7.4 to 2.5 relapses out of 100 people per year.

How the Media Responded

Woloshin and Schwartz analyzed each of the five stories on Tysabri that appeared in the top 20 U.S. newspapers when the approval was announced[10] (see Figure 5-4). Four out of five stories characterized the accelerated approval process as meaning "extra promise" rather than "extra uncertainty" about benefit, said Woloshin. Articles that quantified the treatment effect generally used relative risk numbers, rather than absolute risk, just as in the FDA press release. None mentioned the disability outcome, and none talked about how the drug compares to other drugs on the market in terms of harms. These factors also were not mentioned in the FDA press release.

Effect of Press Releases on Media Coverage

Schwartz presented an argument for using the press release to communicate about uncertainty as well as benefit. Evidence shows that press releases can influence media reporting. Schwartz and Woloshin compared medical journal press releases with news coverage and showed a strong association between what was in the press release and what appeared in the subsequent news stories (Schwartz et al., 2012). Relating these results

---

[10] Due to time constraints, the study used a limited sample. Results are preliminary.

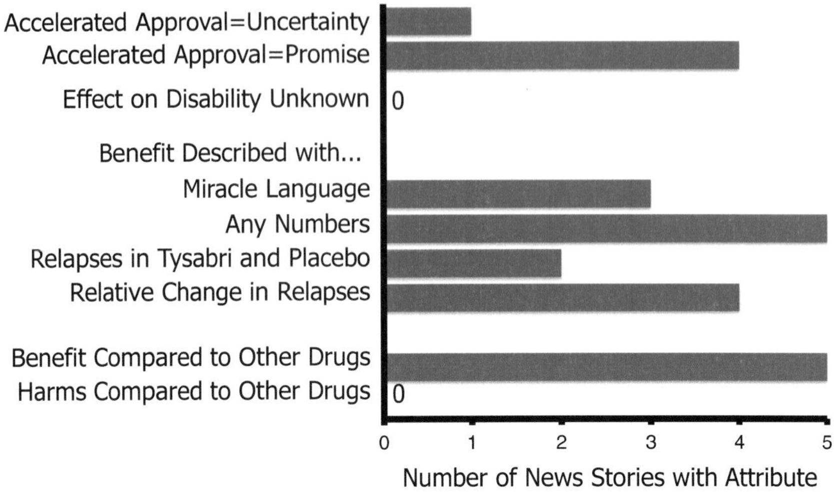

FIGURE 5-4 Media response to 2004 Tysabri approval announcement. Media coverage of the original Tysabri approval largely mirrored the statements and characterizations of the drug's benefit from the FDA press release.
SOURCE: Schwartz and Woloshin, 2014. Presentation at the IOM workshop series on Characterizing and Communicating Uncertainty in the Assessment of Benefits and Risks of Pharmaceutical Products.

to the Tysabri case study, Schwartz noted that FDA issued another press release at the time Tysabri was withdrawn from the market in 2005:

> During the review of Tysabri for remarketing approval, FDA conducted an intensive analysis of possible adverse events that might be related to the effect of the drug on the immune system. No cases of PML were seen in the clinical trials. However, for any approved therapy, new and unexpected adverse events may occur that were not seen in clinical trials.

The final sentence of this excerpt is a great warning, according to Schwartz. However, she added, this statement would be more effective in a press release at the time of approval, rather than after the unexpected adverse effect happens.

FDA could improve communication about uncertainty by being more proactive about communicating the benefits, risks, and uncertainties of a newly approved drug, Schwartz argued. Developing fair presentations of the data and including them consistently in press releases would help all decision makers—patients, providers, lawmakers, and payers.

CHALLENGES AND OPPORTUNITIES TO IMPROVE COMMUNICATION ABOUT UNCERTAINTY[11]

Carmen Bozic, Senior Vice President, Clinical and Safety Sciences, Biogen Idec; Robert Fox, Staff Neurologist, Mellen Center for Multiple Sclerosis and Vice-Chair for Research of the Neurological Institute, Cleveland Clinic; Alice Hughes, Deputy Director for Safety, Division of Neurology, CDER, FDA; Joyce Korvick, Deputy Director for Safety, Division of Gastroenterology and Inborn Error Products, Office of Drug Evaluation III, CDER, FDA; and Cynthia Sitcov, Patient Representative & Voting Member, FDA Central and Peripheral Systems Advisory Committee, participated in a panel discussion moderated by Gavin Huntley-Fenner, Human Factors and Safety Consultant, Huntley-Fenner Advisors, about the challenges and opportunities to improve communication about uncertainty. Patients, providers, the pharmaceutical development industry, and regulators often have different needs and expectations for communications regarding uncertainty about pharmaceutical products.

Balancing Benefits, Risks, and Uncertainties

Balancing what is known about the benefits, risks, and uncertainties of a new drug compared to older drugs with a longer track record is a complex task, highly dependent on the preferences and context for individual patients. The panel discussed the therapeutic environment for MS at the time Tysabri was approved in 2004 and the fact that there was a considerable level of optimism about the high level of effectiveness Tysabri offered in comparison to older MS treatments with a modest level of benefit. In 2004, the significant PML safety concern that would eventually arise was still an "unknown unknown."

Fox suggested that his experience treating MS patients after Tysabri's initial approval has changed his approach to conveying information to patients. In 2004, given the limited availability of other treatment options, he was comfortable recommending Tysabri as a highly effective therapy that seemed safe. Today, with a total of 10 FDA-approved MS therapies on the market, Fox generally suggests 2 or 3 therapeutic options for each

[11] This section is based on the remarks by Carmen Bozic, Senior Vice President, Clinical and Safety Sciences, Biogen Idec; Robert Fox, Staff Neurologist, Mellen Center for Multiple Sclerosis and Vice-Chair for Research of the Neurological Institute, Cleveland Clinic; Alice Hughes, Deputy Director for Safety, Division of Neurology, CDER, FDA; Gavin Huntley-Fenner, Human Factors and Safety Consultant, Huntley-Fenner Advisors; Joyce Korvick, Deputy Director for Safety, Division of Gastroenterology and Inborn Error Products, Office of Drug Evaluation III, CDER, FDA; and Cynthia Sitcov, Patient Representative & Voting Member, FDA Central and Peripheral Systems Advisory Committee.

patient, tailored to their disease severity and treatment preferences. Fox noted that he is sure to explain to patients the extra uncertainty inherent in products that are new to the market, but, he added, this discussion also poses a challenge to the physician–patient relationship. Patients often interpret that the doctor is unknowledgeable instead of "there is uncertainty around this drug," which are two very different things. Patients come to physicians for answers and often do not want to hear explanations about uncertainty around a drug.

Sitcov noted that as a Patient Representative & Voting Member of the FDA Central and Peripheral Systems Advisory Committee who reviewed evidence prior to the remarket authorization of Tysabri, and as an individual with MS, she had to consider the benefits of Tysabri in spite of the risks. Sitcov reflected on the overwhelming testimony from Tysabri users pleading for reapproval of the drug despite its risks. While Sitcov decided against using Tysabri herself, she considered the powerful testimony of a number of patients as she voted to reapprove the drug for the market. Hughes reflected on FDA's decision to remarket Tysabri in 2006 and the careful communication strategy deployed by the agency to characterize the significant level of uncertainty that still remained about the risk of PML and Tysabri.

Fox discussed a risk tolerance study that showed a broad range of maximum risk tolerated by patients for the exact same disease (Fox et al., 2011). The Internet-based study included 5,446 patient volunteers and was conducted through the NARCOMS MS patient registry (a voluntary MS patient registry). The risk tolerance covered the spectrum of "no matter what the risks are, I would still take the treatment" to "regardless, if there was any risk of that, I would not take the treatment." In this study, patients indicated a higher risk tolerance as the severity of their disease increased.

Bozic emphasized the importance of open communication, saying, "Every time we learned something new, we should share it with the regulators, we would share it with prescribers and patients, and we did it through multiple avenues, with the label being the primary approach."

Stephen Sun, Chief Medical Officer, ParagonRx, discussed the management of uncertainties in benefit and risk assessments and suggested that (1) systematic approaches should be used for risk management, (2) a benefit lexicon should be established and could include a benefits table to accompany the adverse events table in a medical product's package insert, and (3) the context in which medical products are used matters and could be better understood with individual stakeholder mapping.

Communication Tools and Quantification of Risk

Regulatory tools for communicating benefits, risks, and uncertainty surrounding a drug include labeling updates, drug safety communications, medication guides, and press releases, said Korvick and Hughes. According to Hughes, FDA issued drug safety communications as the primary communication tool when the agency thought it had information that might change or meaningfully inform discussions and decisions regarding initiation and continuing treatment for individual patients. FDA has wanted to be "transparent, but convey useful, interpretable information that will allow meaningful risk–benefit decisions." Hughes highlighted that the key is to communicate with deliberate statements about the knowns and unknowns of a therapy.

FDA relied on the label as its primary communication tool with prescribers prior to and during the reauthorization of Tysabri because it provided a format to convey a significant amount of detailed information in a meaningful way. However, Hughes noted, given the workshop discussions regarding the importance of information presented in press releases, there might be better options to communicate uncertainty to prescribers.

As part of the REMS requirements following the remarketing of Tysabri, the medication guide was required to be provided to patients during each infusion of the drug. Hughes indicated that although FDA included quantitative estimates of PML incidence in information designed for prescribers (e.g., the label), this quantification of risk was not included in Tysabri's medication guide provided to patients as part of REMS. Hughes suggested that the thinking behind this approach was that the quantification of PML risk would change over time and a quantitative risk discussion was best suited for the patient–physician interaction. Korvick noted the difficulty in conveying risk and uncertainty in the postmarketing setting because calculations of risk often lack a robust denominator reflecting the widespread use of a drug among patients.

Beyond labeling, said Bozic, industry uses other resources to communicate with patients and providers, including medical information channels, websites, and medical science liaisons. Bozic stressed that industry needs to be attentive to communicating a balance of benefit and risk information because patients and physicians have both indicated the desire to receive this balanced information to inform the decision-making process. Building on the workshop discussions earlier in the day regarding patients' ability to understand quantitative estimates, Bozic and Robert Temple, Deputy Director for Clinical Science, and Acting Deputy Director, Office of Drug Evaluation I, CDER, FDA, suggested that industry and regulators could explore opportunities to include meaningful quantification of benefit and risk into medication guides and other communication tools.

6

Final Reflections on Ways to Characterize and Communicate Uncertainty

Key Messages Identified by Individual Speakers

- A research agenda could address questions and focus energy and resources on how best to clinically, methodologically, and statistically reduce uncertainty. Such an agenda could include identifying a scientifically acceptable method to bridge the gap between randomized trials and observational studies.
- A taxonomy of uncertainties could bring structure to thinking about the sources, timing, and impact of uncertainties.
- Social science and qualitative methods to better understand the experience of patients and their medicines could provide a unique opportunity to enrich the context for the regulatory decision maker.
- Patients and providers could benefit from receiving quantitative information on benefits and risks of pharmaceutical products, as well as clear statements about inherent uncertainties.

As part of the final session of the May 12, 2014, workshop, several speakers and workshop participants reflected on what they had heard over the course of the workshops. Their ideas are gathered in this final chapter as a way to highlight and elaborate on potential next steps for improving the characterization and communication of uncertainty in benefit–risk assessments of pharmaceutical products.

IDENTIFYING AND MITIGATING UNCERTAINTY THROUGH MAXIMIZING THE VALUE OF EVIDENCE

Many FDA workshop participants noted that federal laws and regulations provide the boundaries for FDA's decisions about drug approvals and that, by statute, FDA can tolerate less uncertainty about efficacy than about safety or harms. Drawing conclusions in the regulatory setting, in the midst of uncertainty, is a challenging task that might be made more efficient and transparent with the implementation of systematic approaches to dealing with uncertainty.

There is a need for a *research agenda* to address questions and focus energy and resources on how best to clinically, methodologically, and statistically reduce uncertainty, noted Paul J. Seligman, Executive Director, U.S. Regulatory Policy, Amgen Inc. Such a research agenda could include finding a scientifically acceptable method to bridge the gap between randomized trials, which are focused on proving drug efficacy in a study population, and observational studies, which focus on risk and adverse events in the real world. Seligman referenced the presentation by Sebastian Schneeweiss of Harvard Medical School (see Figure 2-1) and the opportunity to structure a clinical trial portfolio to use multiple studies with different designs and data sources to reduce uncertainty. Multiple studies could be optimally arranged to reduce chance, better characterize representativeness, and reduce bias with the hope that the resulting information would be timely, valid, and comprehensive for decision makers. Taking a structured approach to designing multiple clinical trials could also be a more efficient use of resources. Statistical techniques such as sensitivity analyses can also help to make better use of the data collected and further characterize uncertainty. Several workshop participants also referenced the work of the Innovative Medicines Initiative (IMI) Pharmacoepidemiological Research on Outcomes of Therapeutics by a European Consortium (PROTECT) to study and address limitations of current methods in the fields of pharmacoepidemiology and pharmacovigilance.[1]

Several workshop participants also highlighted "low-hanging fruit" opportunities to improve the value of evidence generated from clinical trials to reduce uncertainty. In summarizing the presentations and discussions from the February 12 workshop, Seligman indicated that *maximizing the utility of clinical trial data* could include ensuring all clinical trials and studies are registered on ClinicalTrials.gov, consistently naming the products being studied in government databases and the scientific literature so

[1] For more information on Innovative Medicines Initiative (IMI) Pharmacoepidemiological Research on Outcomes of Therapeutics by a European Consortium (PROTECT), see http://www.imi-protect.eu (accessed September 18, 2014).

that all studies for a particular product can be easily identified and used, and working to keep patients in trials and following up with those who leave a trial to increase retention and reduce the uncertainty of a trial's results.

Ralph I. Horwitz, Senior Vice President, Clinical Sciences Evaluation, GlaxoSmithKline, suggested expanding the scope of information used in regulatory decisions to include not just the traditional placebo-controlled efficacy trials, but *pragmatic trials* that provide richer information about how a drug might actually be used in clinical settings. John Jenkins, Director, Office of New Drugs, CDER, FDA, indicated that FDA supports the elimination of unnecessary exclusion criteria in clinical trials to bring the information closer to what patients would experience in the real world.

CHARACTERIZING AND UNDERSTANDING UNCERTAINTIES

A clear *taxonomy of uncertainties* that describes the nature of information gaps, their effects, and the steps that need to be taken to address those information gaps could improve the characterization and understanding of uncertainties, noted Seligman. Such a taxonomy could also bring structure to thinking about the sources, timing, and impact of uncertainties.

Bayesian approaches to evaluating clinical trial data have the potential for more robust characterization of inferences drawn from studies, said Seligman. A disciplined Bayesian approach offers opportunities to characterize and accommodate uncertainty in clinical trials. Bennett Levitan, Director of Quantitative Safety Research, Department of Epidemiology, Johnson & Johnson, noted that additional research is needed on the potential of Bayesian approaches to combine data from multiple clinical trials (e.g., an RCT and observational study if the necessary variables are contained in each). Levitan further explained that Bayesian methods might allow different stakeholders to embed their preferences in the analysis of trials by virtue of having a prior distribution from one group versus another. To move from idea to practice, Levitan suggested that FDA could help spur research from industry and academia on Bayesian methods to better characterize uncertainty in evidence from clinical trials.

ELICITING VALUES FROM STAKEHOLDERS, PARTICULARLY PATIENTS

Horwitz suggested there is a need to formalize the personal experience of patients with medicines in the pre- and postapproval periods. He suggested including *social science and qualitative methods* to better understand the experience of patients and their medicines to provide context for the regulator.

With the support of FDA, *PRO instruments* are increasingly being included in clinical trials to measure the effect of a medical intervention on one or more concepts (e.g., a symptom or group of symptoms). Some workshop participants suggested that there could be an important role for patient groups to develop PRO instruments outside of the regulatory process for a particular product and ideally before a new drug is contemplated for development. PFDD meetings could serve as one platform for patient groups to gather the information to support the development of a PRO instrument. In addition, one workshop participant suggested that if multiple pharmaceutical companies had an interest in discovery and development activities for a particular disease or condition, they could pool funding to have an independent patient group develop the PRO instrument to be shared by all.

Some workshop participants also explained a "*risk-risk*" concept for patients when considering whether or not to take a drug. Benefit is traditionally understood as an additional advantage or bonus, but the "benefit" of taking a drug could actually be understood as avoiding the harms and adverse experiences of a disease. Thus, patients weigh the risks, and inherent uncertainties, of experiencing adverse effects from their disease versus the risks, and inherent uncertainties of experiencing adverse effects of the treatment.

Schneeweiss suggested developing a *metric* to compare evidence on benefits and harms that incorporates patient preferences. Such a metric would ideally be informed by greater reporting of actual risk differences and relative risk. Schneeweiss explained that this risk information is retrievable from studies submitted to FDA for regulatory approval, but should be presented in a more accessible way. This information, coupled with patient preferences, could inform the development of a metric to help weigh benefits and harms.

FDA might also consider novel ways to elicit expert advice. Seligman noted that he knows of no other federal agency that seeks as much expert advice as FDA through the public advisory committee function. The science of *expert elicitation* could offer new opportunities for FDA to develop systematic ways of gathering expert input (i.e., methods that differ from going around the table to solicit advice during a public advisory committee meeting).

COMMUNICATING UNCERTAINTY ABOUT BENEFIT AND RISK ASSESSMENTS OF PHARMACEUTICAL PRODUCTS

In addition to the importance of identifying and communicating sources of uncertainty in clinical data, Robert Temple of FDA noted that FDA could do better in presenting the important data already on hand.

For instance, product labels currently do not, but could, include information about the *effect of a treatment on subgroups* (e.g., treatment effect by age, race, and sex) so that patients can gain a better understanding of how the treatment might work for them based on certain characteristics. FDA has this subgroup information, but usually does not include it in the product label unless it contains a striking or unusual finding. Temple also suggested that treatment effect data by subgroup should not be limited to studies of treatments for conditions that lend themselves more easily to hard outcomes (e.g., CV disease and mortality), but should also be provided for conditions such as depression.

A number of workshop participants noted the *limitations of language* in its ability to communicate accurate information. David R. Mandel of DRDC presented a corrective measure in the form of a prohibition on "weasel words" and phrases, such as "reportedly," "evidence suggests (or indicates)," "distinctly possible," and "apparently." Such uncertain words are not well suited to the complex task of communicating uncertainty about benefit–risk assessments in pharmaceutical products.

Some workshop participants discussed the idea that *conveying information numerically* can provide greater clarity, but also presents its own challenges. For instance, Temple stated that providing the mean result for a depression score is not very informative because individuals experience a range of treatment effects varying widely from the average result. According to Temple, FDA is increasing its reporting of the cumulative distribution of results, such as the number of people who experience a 10, 20, 30, or 40 percent improvement in their condition as a result of the treatment. Reporting this variability enriches the communication about a drug and helps patients better understand the likelihood that they will benefit from a particular drug.

Lisa M. Schwartz, Dartmouth Medical School and Center for Medicine and the Media at The Dartmouth Institute for Health Policy and Clinical Practice, and Steven Woloshin, Dartmouth Medical School and Center for Medicine and the Media at The Dartmouth Institute for Health Policy and Clinical Practice, suggested FDA adopt a quantitative format for conveying benefit and risk information that includes the base rate. For example, compared to placebo, the drug reduced the relapse rate from 7.4 relapses per 100 people per year to 2.5 relapses per 100 people per year. This quantification gives readers a better understanding of the drug's benefits than does simply providing a relative risk reduction (e.g., the drug reduced the frequency of relapses by 66 percent relative to placebo), which can exaggerate the perceived benefits. Levitan suggested FDA consider including an effects table that contains benefit and harm information in the same unit of measurement. Including this comparison in a prominent section of the product label could improve interpretability of benefit–harm information and patient and physician decision making, noted Levitan. The EMA is piloting the use of an effects table as a tool to summarize key benefits and risks in the review process.[2]

FDA has a number of *communication tools* currently in its arsenal for conveying information to a broad range of stakeholders. Patrick J. Frey of FDA indicated that as part of FDA's implementation of the benefit–risk framework, the agency can consider opportunities to improve how it currently communicates information about benefit, risk, and uncertainty when posting review documents on the FDA website. As the new framework is implemented, the agency will have the chance to further optimize communications about the rationale behind regulatory decisions.

---

[2] For more information on the EMA's Benefit–Risk Methodology Project, see http://www.ema.europa.eu/docs/en_GB/document_library/Report/2011/07/WC500109477.pdf (accessed September 18, 2014).

References

Berlin, J. A., B. J. Crowe, E. Whalen, H. A. Xia, C. E. Koro, and J. Kuebler. 2012. Meta-analysis of clinical trial safety data in a drug development program: Answers to frequently asked questions. *Clinical Trials* 10:20-31.

Downing, N. S., J. A. Aminawung, N. D. Shah, H. M. Krumholz, and J. S. Ross. 2014. Clinical trial evidence supporting FDA approval of novel therapeutic agents, 2005-2012. *Journal of the American Medical Association* 311(4):368-377.

Eichler, H. G., K. Oye, L. G. Baird, E. Abadie, J. Brown, C. L. Drum, J. Ferguson, S. Garner, P. Honig, M. Hukkelhoven, J. C. W. Lim, R. Lim, M. M. Lumpkin, G. Neil, B. O'Rourke, E. Pezalla, D. Shoda, V. Seyfert-Margolis, E. V. Sigal, J. Sobotka, D. Tan, T. F. Unger, and G. Hirsch. 2012. Adaptive licensing: Taking the next step in the evolution of drug approval. *Clinical Pharmacology & Therapeutics* 91(3):426-437.

Eichler, H. G., B. Bloechl-Daum, D. Brasseur, A. Breckenridge, H. Leufkens, J. Raine, T. Salmonson, C. K. Schneider, and G. Rasi. 2013. The risks of risk aversion in drug regulation. *Nature Reviews Drug Discovery* 12(12):907-916.

FDA (U.S. Food and Drug Administration). 2004 (November 23). *First monoclonal antibody treatment for multiple sclerosis approved*. Press release. Washington, DC: FDA.

FDA. 2009a. Guidance for industry: Format and content of proposed Risk Evaluation and Mitigation Strategies (REMS), REMS assessments, and proposed REMS modifications—Draft guidance. http://www.fda.gov/downloads/Drugs/GuidanceCompliance RegulatoryInformation/Guidances/UCM184128.pdf (accessed September 11, 2014).

FDA. 2009b. Minutes of the Risk Communication Advisory Committee, FDA. http://www.fda.gov/downloads/advisorycommittees/committeesmeetingmaterials/risk communicationadvisorycommittee/ucm152593.pdf (accessed September 11, 2014).

FDA. 2013. *Structured approach to benefit–risk assessment in drug regulatory decision-making: Draft PDUFA V Implementation Plan—February 2013, Fiscal Years 2013-2017*. http://patientnetwork.fda.gov/sites/default/files/fda_benefit-risk_draft_plan_final_for_posting.pdf (accessed August 18, 2014).

FDA. 2014. Guidance for industry: Labeling for human prescription drug and biological products approved under the accelerated approval regulatory pathway. http://www.fda.gov/downloads/Drugs/GuidanceComplianceRegulatoryInformation/Guidances/UCM390058.pdf (accessed September 11, 2014).

Fox, R., A. Salter, J. M. Alster, N. V. Dawson, S. Johnson, M. Kattan, D. Miller, T. Tyry, T. Vollmer, B. Wells, and G. Cutter. 2011. *Risk tolerance in MS patients: Survey results from the NARCOMS Registry*. American Academy of Neurology Annual Meeting, April 2011, Honolulu, Hawaii.

Frey, P. 2014. *Case studies of uncertainty in the assessment of benefits and risks*. Presentation at the IOM workshop series on Characterizing and Communicating Uncertainty in the Assessment of Benefits and Risks of Pharmaceutical Products, February 12 and May 12, White Oak, Maryland.

Gagne, J. J., S. V. Wang, J. A. Rassen, and S. Schneeweiss. 2014. A modular, prospective, semi-automated drug safety monitoring system for use in a distributed data environment. *Pharmacoepidemiology and Drug Safety* 23:619-627.

Hammad, T. A., S. P. Pinheiro, and G. A. Neyarapally. 2011. Secondary use of randomized controlled trials to evaluate drug safety: A review of methodological considerations. *Clinical Trials* 8(5):559-570.

Hammad, T. A., G. A. Neyarapally, S. Iyasu, J. A. Staffa, and G. Dal Pan. 2013. The future of population-based postmarket drug risk assessment: A regulator's perspective. *Clinical Pharmacology & Therapeutics* 94(3):349-358.

IOM (Institute of Medicine). 2007. *The future of drug safety: Promoting and protecting the health of the public*. Washington, DC: The National Academies Press.

IOM. 2014. *Characterizing uncertainty in the assessment of benefits and risks of pharmaceutical products*, Workshop in Brief, Institute of Medicine, Washington, DC.

Krishnamurti, T., S. L. Eggers, and B. Fischhoff. 2008. The impact of over-the-counter availability of "Plan B" on teens' contraceptive decision making. *Social Science & Medicine* 67(4):618-627.

Lim, R. 2014. *A regulatory approach to uncertainty for the "real world."* Presentation at the IOM workshop series on Characterizing and Communicating Uncertainty in the Assessment of Benefits and Risks of Pharmaceutical Products, February 12 and May 12, White Oak, Maryland.

Mandel, D. R. 2007. *Toward a concept of risk for effective military decision making*. Defence Research and Development Canada, Toronto Technical Report 2007-124. Toronto, Canada: Defence Research and Development Canada. http://cradpdf.drdc-rddc.gc.ca/PDFS/unc68/p529014.pdf (accessed August 23, 2014).

Parks, M. 2014. *Challenges to the regulator in communicating uncertainties in risks of approved pharmaceuticals*. Presentation at the IOM workshop series on Characterizing and Communicating Uncertainty in the Assessment of Benefits and Risks of Pharmaceutical Products, February 12 and May 12, White Oak, Maryland.

Savovic, J., H. E. Jones, D. G. Altman, R. J. Harris, P. Juni, J. Pildal, B. Als-Nielsen, E. M. Balk, C. Gluud, L. Lotte Gluud, J. P. A. Ioannidis, K. F. Schulz, R. Beynon, N. J. Welton, L. Wood, D. Moher, J. J. Deeks, and J. A. C. Sterne. 2012. Influence of reported study design characteristics on intervention effect estimates from randomized controlled trials. *Annals of Internal Medicine* 157:429-438.

Schneeweiss, S. 2014. *Addressing uncertainties in the evaluation of pharmaceutical benefits and harms during the market access phase*. Presentation at the IOM workshop series on Characterizing and Communicating Uncertainty in the Assessment of Benefits and Risks of Pharmaceutical Products, February 12 and May 12, White Oak, Maryland.

Schwartz, L. M, and S. Woloshin. 2011. Communicating uncertainties about prescription drugs to the public: A national randomized trial. *JAMA Archives of Internal Medicine* 171(16):1463-1468.

Schwartz, L. M., and S. Woloshin. 2013. The drug facts box: Improving the communication of prescription drug information. *Proceedings of the National Academy of Sciences of the United States of America* 110:14069-14074.

Schwartz, L. M., and S. Woloshin. 2014. *Media analysis: Tysabri case study*. Presentation at the IOM workshop series on Characterizing and Communicating Uncertainty in the Assessment of Benefits and Risks of Pharmaceutical Products, February 12 and May 12, White Oak, Maryland.

Schwartz, L. M., S. Woloshin, A. Andrews, and T. Stukel. 2012. Influence of medical journal press releases on the quality of associated newspaper coverage: retrospective cohort study. *British Medical Journal*. http://www.bmj.com/content/bmj/344/bmj.d8164.full.pdf (accessed September 8, 2014).

Tamura, R. N., D. E. Faries, J. S. Andersen, and J. H. Heiligenstein. 1994. A case study of an adaptive clinical trial in the treatment of out-patients with depressive disorder. *Journal of the American Statistical Association* 89:768-776.

Appendix A

Workshop Agenda

CHARACTERIZING AND COMMUNICATING UNCERTAINTY IN THE ASSESSMENT OF BENEFITS AND RISKS OF PHARMACEUTICAL PRODUCTS: AN INSTITUTE OF MEDICINE WORKSHOP

February 12, 2014
U.S. Food and Drug Administration (FDA) Campus
White Oak, Maryland

Background and Meeting Objectives

There is increasing attention on the need for enhancing the evaluation and communication of the benefits and risks associated with pharmaceutical products, thereby increasing the predictability, transparency, and efficiency of pharmaceutical regulatory decision making. In 2006, the IOM's Forum on Drug Discovery, Development, and Translation held a workshop to explore the complex trade-off between drug benefits and risks and to examine approaches for better quantifying this balance and informing the public and the medical community. Since that time, FDA has worked to develop an enhanced structured approach to the assessment of benefits and risks in drug regulatory decision making to better communicate this aspect of the human drug review process. FDA envisions that this framework will serve as a template for product reviews, as well as a vehicle for explaining the basis for FDA's regulatory decisions.[1] FDA's work in this area coincides with efforts by other regulatory agencies, academia, and the pharmaceutical industry.

As FDA's draft PDUFA V Implementation Plan (the Plan) indicates, an extensive body of evidence informs regulatory decisions on the safety and efficacy of a proposed product, but in many cases, FDA must draw conclusions from imperfect data. Identifying and evaluating sources of uncertainty (e.g., absence of information, conflicting findings, marginal results) in a regulatory application is an important part of reviewers' work; however, drawing conclusions in the face of uncertainty can be a complex and challenging task. Effectively communicating regulatory decisions necessarily includes explanation of the impact of uncertainty on decision making. Uncertainty may arise from many sources; however, two particular areas of uncertainty that could benefit from additional attention are (1) the translation of premarket clinical trial data to the postmarket setting in which an approved drug is used in a much wider patient population, and (2) new findings that emerge in a postmarketing setting where the basis for the finding comes from sources of varying levels of rigor.

This public workshop will address the opportunity to advance the development of more systematic and structured approaches to characterize and communicate (a) the sources of uncertainty in the assessment of benefits and risks; and (b) their implications for pharmaceutical regulatory decisions. Specifically, the workshop will explore potential analytical and communication approaches and identify key considerations on their development, evaluation, and incorporation into the assessment of benefits and risks in pharmaceuticals. This workshop will consider the entire drug development lifecycle, including premarket drug review and postmarket safety surveillance.

The workshop objectives are to:

- Discuss the challenges in applying more systematic approaches to characterizing and communicating uncertainty in the assessment of a drug's benefits and risks.
- Identify potential systematic approaches to address uncertainty faced by regulators in the assessment of benefits and risks in pharmaceuticals, drawing from various scientific and regulatory disciplines and domains.

[1] FDA's structured approach to benefit–risk assessment in drug regulatory decision making is outlined in the Draft PDUFA V Implementation Plan [February 2013], available at http://www.fda.gov/downloads/ForIndustry/UserFees/PrescriptionDrugUserFee/UCM329758.pdf (accessed August 23, 2014).

- Identify possible principles, best practices, and resources that can facilitate the development, evaluation, and incorporation of such approaches in regulatory decision making.
- Explore principles and approaches to facilitate the communication about uncertainty in the assessment of benefits and risks with FDA stakeholders.

First Workshop in the Series

9:00 a.m. Opening Remarks

BARUCH FISCHHOFF, *Workshop Co-Chair*
Howard Heinz University Professor
Department of Social and Decision Sciences
Department of Engineering and Public Policy
Carnegie Mellon University

ROBERT RATNER, *Workshop Co-Chair*
Chief Scientific and Medical Officer
American Diabetes Association

9:15 a.m. **The Importance of Considering Uncertainty in Regulatory Decision Making** (*15 min.*)

JANET WOODCOCK
Director, Center for Drug Evaluation and Research
U.S. Food and Drug Administration

SESSION I: APPROACHES TO EVALUATE UNCERTAINTY: MAXIMIZING THE VALUE OF THE EVIDENCE

Session Objectives:

- Discuss potential methods (proven and yet to be tried) to identify and evaluate sources of uncertainty. What structured systematic approaches to evaluating uncertainties could be considered by regulators?
- Acknowledge and discuss challenges in both identifying and addressing uncertainty in drug regulation.

9:30 a.m. Background and Session Objectives (*5 min.*)

BARUCH FISCHHOFF, *Workshop Co-Chair*
Howard Heinz University Professor
Department of Social and Decision Sciences
Department of Engineering and Public Policy
Carnegie Mellon University

9:35 a.m. **Key Sources of Uncertainty in the Assessment of Benefits and Risks of Pharmaceuticals and Associated Challenges** (*15 min.*)

TAREK A. HAMMAD
Executive Director, Epidemiology
Merck Research Laboratories
Merck & Co., Inc.

9:50 a.m. Identifying and Evaluating Uncertainty

Addressing Challenges Arising from the Completeness of Data Collection in Clinical Trials (*15 min.*)

DEBORAH A. ZARIN
Director, ClinicalTrials.gov
National Library of Medicine
National Institutes of Health

Identifying and Retaining Subgroups in Clinical Trials in the Context of Uncertainty About the External Validity of Clinical Trials (*15 min.*)

MICHAELA KIERNAN
Senior Research Scientist
Stanford Prevention Research Center
Stanford University School of Medicine

Research Methodologies to Reduce or Address Uncertainties in the Evaluation of Pharmaceutical Benefits and Risks (*15 min.*)

SEBASTIAN SCHNEEWEISS
Professor of Medicine and Epidemiology
Harvard Medical School

10:35 a.m. Discussion with Speakers and Audience (*20 min.*)

Discussion Moderator: Brian Strom, Chancellor, Biomedical and Health Sciences, Rutgers University

10:55 a.m. **BREAK** (*15 min.*)

SESSION II: CASE STUDIES: UNCERTAINTY IN THE ASSESSMENT OF BENEFITS AND RISKS OF PHARMACEUTICAL PRODUCTS

Session Objectives:

- Provide an overview of FDA's approach to evaluating benefits and risks of pharmaceutical products and how these approaches take into consideration sources of uncertainty.
- Identify a range of uncertainties faced by drug regulators through presentation of two drug product case studies from FDA, including pre- and postmarket experiences. The case studies will illustrate how the uncertainty was considered and addressed in the decision-making process within the constraints of protecting proprietary information.

11:10 a.m. Background and Session Objectives (*5 min.*)

PATRICK FREY, *Session Chair*
Director, Office of Program and Strategic Analysis
Center for Drug Evaluation and Research
U.S. Food and Drug Administration

11:15 a.m. **FDA Approach to Evaluating Benefits and Risks of Pharmaceuticals** (*10 min.*)

PATRICK FREY
Director, Office of Program and Strategic Analysis
Center for Drug Evaluation and Research
U.S. Food and Drug Administration

11:25 a.m. Presentation of FDA Case Studies

Tysabri (natalizumab)/Multiple Sclerosis (MS) (*15 min.*)

ROBERT TEMPLE
Deputy Director for Clinical Science
Acting Deputy Director, Office of Drug Evaluation I
Center for Drug Evaluation and Research
U.S. Food and Drug Administration

Anoro Ellipta (umeclidinium and vilanterol inhalation powder)/Chronic Obstructive Pulmonary Disease (COPD) (*15 min.*)

JENNIFER PIPPINS
Medical Officer
Division of Pulmonary, Allergy, and Rheumatology Products
Center for Drug Evaluation and Research
U.S. Food and Drug Administration

11:55 a.m. Discussion with Speakers and Audience (*15 min.*)

Discussion Moderator: Patrick Frey, Director, Office of Program and Strategic Analysis, Center for Drug Evaluation and Research, U.S. Food and Drug Administration

12:10 p.m. **LUNCH** (*50 min.*)

SESSION III: METHODS TO ADDRESS UNCERTAINTY: MAKING SENSE OF FINDINGS FROM THE EVIDENCE

Session Objectives:

- Consider methods, statistical or otherwise, that could be deployed by the regulator to evaluate and address issues of uncertainty in clinical research data.
- Present methods, approaches, and lessons learned from other regulatory domains, which could address the challenges of identification and evaluation of uncertainty in regulatory decision making.

1:00 p.m. Background and Session Objectives (*5 min.*)

Baruch Fischhoff, *Workshop Co-Chair*
Howard Heinz University Professor
Department of Social and Decision Sciences
Department of Engineering and Public Policy
Carnegie Mellon University

1:05 p.m. **Methods to Characterize and Elicit Uncertainty** (*15 min.*)

M. Granger Morgan [*via remote presentation*]
Professor and Head
Department of Engineering and Public Policy
Carnegie Mellon University

1:20 p.m. Addressing Challenges of Identification and Evaluation of Uncertainty

Experiences in Implementing Uncertainty Assessments in the Defense/Intelligence Communities (*15 min.*)

David R. Mandel
Senior Scientist
Defence Research and Development Canada, Toronto Research Centre

Systematic Approaches to Assessing the Internal and External Validity of Randomized Controlled Trials (*15 min.*)

John P. A. Ioannidis [*via remote presentation*]
C.F. Rehnborg Professor in Disease Prevention
Professor of Health Research and Policy
Stanford University School of Medicine

Bayesian Approaches to Evaluating Clinical Trial Data (*15 min.*)

Joel Greenhouse
Professor of Statistics
Carnegie Mellon University

2:05 p.m. Discussion with Speakers and Audience (*20 min.*)

Discussion Moderator: Lisa LaVange, Director, Office of Biostatistics, Office of Translational Sciences, Center for Drug Evaluation and Research, U.S. Food and Drug Administration

2:25 p.m. **BREAK** (*15 min.*)

SESSION IV: REGULATORY DECISION MAKING UNDER UNCERTAINTY

Session Objective:

- Discuss potential approaches from decision theory that could be used in the regulatory setting (e.g., case studies), acknowledging that approaches will vary in the context of the unique uncertainties presented and that ultimately, the regulator will need to decide.

2:40 p.m. Background and Session Objective (*5 min.*)

Baruch Fischhoff, *Workshop Co-Chair*
Howard Heinz University Professor
Department of Social and Decision Sciences
Department of Engineering and Public Policy
Carnegie Mellon University

2:45 p.m. **Public Policy in an Uncertain World: Analysis and Decisions in Pharmaceutical Benefits and Risks** (*15 min.*)

Charles F. Manski
Board of Trustees Professor in Economics
Northwestern University

3:00 p.m. Approaches Suggested from Decision Theory to Support Regulatory Decision Making Under Uncertainty

Approaches to Eliciting Values for Uncertain Choices (*15 min.*)

Timothy McDaniels
Faculty of Science
Institute of Resources and Environment
University of British Columbia

Consultative Processes for Acceptable Decisions (*15 min.*)

JOSEPH ARVAI
Svare Chair in Applied Decision Research
Department of Geography
Institute for Sustainable Energy, Environment, and Economy
University of Calgary

3:30 p.m. Discussion with Speakers and Audience (*20 min.*)

Discussion Moderator: Paul Seligman, Executive Director, U.S. Regulatory Policy, Amgen Inc.

3:50 p.m. **Public Comment Period** (*30 min.*)

SESSION V: CONSIDERATIONS ON IMPLEMENTING STRUCTURED APPROACHES TO CHARACTERIZING UNCERTAINTY

Session Objectives:

- Reflecting on the presentations and discussions of the day, identify and discuss possible principles and best practices to successfully implement structured approaches to address uncertainty in the assessment of pharmaceutical benefits and risks.
- Consider the culture and institutional support needed to advance the development, evaluation, and incorporation of structured approaches to evaluate uncertainty in the regulatory decision-making process.

4:20 p.m. Background and Session Objectives (*5 min.*)

BARUCH FISCHHOFF, *Workshop Co-Chair*
Howard Heinz University Professor
Department of Social and Decision Sciences
Department of Engineering and Public Policy
Carnegie Mellon University

4:25 p.m. **Reaction Panel and Discussion with the Audience: Decision Making in the Context of Uncertainty** (*35 min.*)

FRANCESCO PIGNATTI
Oncology, Hematology, Diagnostics Section
Scientific and Regulatory Management Department
European Medicines Agency

KIMBY BARTON
Director, Bureau of Cardiology, Allergy, and Neurological Sciences
Health Canada

JOHN JENKINS
Director, Office of New Drugs
Center for Drug Evaluation and Research
U.S. Food and Drug Administration

RALPH HORWITZ
Senior Vice President
Clinical Sciences Evaluation
GlaxoSmithKline

TIMOTHY MCDANIELS
Faculty of Science
Institute of Resources and Environment
University of British Columbia

Panel and Discussion Moderator: Baruch Fischhoff, Howard Heinz University Professor, Department of Social and Decision Sciences, Department of Engineering and Public Policy, Carnegie Mellon University

5:00 p.m. Adjourn

CHARACTERIZING AND COMMUNICATING UNCERTAINTY IN THE ASSESSMENT OF BENEFITS AND RISKS OF PHARMACEUTICAL PRODUCTS: AN INSTITUTE OF MEDICINE WORKSHOP

May 12, 2014
U.S. Food and Drug Administration (FDA) Campus
White Oak, Maryland

Background and Meeting Objectives

There is increasing attention on the need for enhancing the evaluation and communication of the benefits and risks associated with pharmaceutical products, thereby increasing the predictability, transparency, and efficiency of pharmaceutical regulatory decision making. In 2006, the IOM's Forum on Drug Discovery, Development, and Translation held a workshop to explore the complex trade-off between drug benefits and risks and to examine approaches for better quantifying this balance and informing the public and the medical community. Since that time, FDA has worked to develop an enhanced structured approach to the assessment of benefits and risks in drug regulatory decision making to better communicate this aspect of the human drug review process. FDA envisions that this framework will serve as a template for product reviews, as well as a vehicle for explaining the basis for FDA's regulatory decisions.[2] FDA's work in this area coincides with efforts by other regulatory agencies, academia, and the pharmaceutical industry.

As FDA's draft PDUFA V Implementation Plan (the Plan) indicates, an extensive body of evidence informs regulatory decisions on the safety and efficacy of a proposed product, but in many cases, FDA must draw conclusions from imperfect data. Identifying and evaluating sources of uncertainty (e.g., absence of information, conflicting findings, marginal results) in a regulatory application is an important part of reviewers' work; however, drawing conclusions in the face of uncertainty can be a complex and challenging task. Effectively communicating regulatory decisions necessarily includes explanation of the impact of uncertainty on decision making. Uncertainty may arise from many sources; however, two particular areas of uncertainty that could benefit from additional attention are (1) the translation of premarket clinical trial data to the postmarket setting in which an approved drug is used in a much wider patient popu-

[2] FDA's structured approach to benefit–risk assessment in drug regulatory decision making is outlined in the Draft PDUFA V Implementation Plan [February 2013], available at http://www.fda.gov/downloads/ForIndustry/UserFees/PrescriptionDrugUserFee/UCM329758.pdf (accessed September 18, 2014).

lation, and (2) new findings that emerge in a postmarketing setting where the basis for the finding comes from sources of varying levels of rigor.

This two-part public workshop series will address the opportunity to advance the development of more systematic and structured approaches to characterize and communicate (a) the sources of uncertainty in the assessment of benefits and risks; and (b) their implications for pharmaceutical regulatory decisions. Specifically, the workshop series will explore potential analytical and communication approaches and identify key considerations on their development, evaluation, and incorporation into the assessment of benefits and risks in pharmaceuticals. This workshop series will consider the entire drug development lifecycle, including premarket drug review and postmarket safety surveillance.

The workshop series objectives are to:

- Discuss the challenges in applying more systematic approaches to characterizing and communicating uncertainty in the assessment of a drug's benefits and risks.
- Identify potential systematic approaches to address uncertainty faced by regulators in the assessment of benefits and risks in pharmaceuticals, drawing from various scientific and regulatory disciplines and domains.
- Identify possible principles, best practices, and resources that can facilitate the development, evaluation, and incorporation of such approaches in regulatory decision making.
- Explore principles and approaches to facilitate the communication about uncertainty in the assessment of benefits and risks with FDA stakeholders.

Second Workshop in the Series

9:00 a.m. Welcome and Opening Remarks

BARUCH FISCHHOFF, *Workshop Co-Chair*
Howard Heinz University Professor
Department of Social and Decision Sciences
Department of Engineering and Public Policy
Carnegie Mellon University

ROBERT RATNER, *Workshop Co-Chair*
Chief Scientific and Medical Officer
American Diabetes Association

SESSION I: REFLECTIONS ON CHARACTERIZING UNCERTAINTY: LESSONS FROM THE FIRST WORKSHOP

Session Objectives:

- Discuss objectives of the first workshop.
- Identify key themes from the first workshop.
- Discuss how lessons and observations from the first workshop could support the advancement of approaches to characterizing uncertainty in the assessment of benefits and risks and their implications for pharmaceutical regulatory decisions.

BARUCH FISCHHOFF, *Workshop Co-Chair, Session Chair*
Howard Heinz University Professor
Department of Social and Decision Sciences
Department of Engineering and Public Policy
Carnegie Mellon University

9:05 a.m. **The Challenge of Uncertainty in Regulatory Decision Making** *(20 min.)*

PATRICK FREY
Director, Office of Program and Strategic Analysis
Center for Drug Evaluation and Research
U.S. Food and Drug Administration

9:25 a.m. **Key Messages and Potential Lessons Learned** *(30 min.)*

BARUCH FISCHHOFF, *Workshop Co-Chair*
Howard Heinz University Professor
Department of Social and Decision Sciences
Department of Engineering and Public Policy
Carnegie Mellon University

PAUL SELIGMAN
Executive Director, U.S. Regulatory Policy
Amgen Inc.

Discussion Question:

- How can the concepts discussed in day 1 be applied and operationalized in characterizing uncertainty in pharmaceutical product evaluation?

9:55 a.m. **BREAK** *(15 min.)*

SESSION II: OVERVIEW OF REGULATORY STRATEGIES ABOUT UNCERTAINTY IN THE BENEFIT AND RISK ASSESSMENT

Session Objectives:

- Provide an overview of regulatory strategies for communicating benefits and risks of pharmaceutical products and clarify the drug regulator's role in communicating uncertainty.
- Discuss FDA's Patient-Focused Drug Development initiative and consider the ways in which FDA receives information from different stakeholders and incorporates this information into addressing the relevant uncertainties in the assessment of benefits and risks.

10:10 a.m. Background and Session Objectives (*5 min.*)

ROBERT RATNER, *Workshop Co-Chair*
Chief Scientific and Medical Officer
American Diabetes Association

10:15 a.m. **Challenges to the Regulator in Communicating Uncertainties in Risks of Approved Pharmaceuticals** (*15 min.*)

MARY H. PARKS
Deputy Director, Office of Drug Evaluation II
Office of New Drugs
Center for Drug Evaluation and Research
U.S. Food and Drug Administration

10:30 a.m. **FDA Patient-Focused Drug Development Initiative** (*15 min.*)

THERESA MULLIN
Director, Office of Strategic Programs
Center for Drug Evaluation and Research
U.S. Food and Drug Administration

10:45 a.m. **Health Canada's Approach to Uncertainty Within Its Benefit–Harm–Uncertainty Initiative** (*15 min.*)

ROBYN LIM
Senior Science Advisor, Office of Legislative and Regulatory Modernization
Health Products and Food Branch
Health Canada

11:00 a.m. Discussion with Speakers and Audience (*20 min.*)

Discussion Moderator: Robert Ratner, Chief Scientific and Medical Officer, American Diabetes Association

Discussion Questions:

- How can the patient voice inform how much uncertainty can be tolerated?
- How do we communicate information about what is known and unknown about benefits and risks as that information changes?

SESSION III: COMMUNICATING UNCERTAINTY ABOUT BENEFIT AND RISK ASSESSMENTS

Session Objectives:

- Understand and consider the implications of the communication of uncertainty about benefit and risk assessments on the health care system beyond drug regulatory decision making.
- Understand a patient perspective on what is important to patients in understanding the assessments of benefit and risk and how patients want to receive and share information about uncertainty.
- Consider methodological challenges in communication strategies and suggest approaches for overcoming the "false precision" that can arise in assigning probabilities to patient outcomes.
- Suggest principles and approaches to improve the communication about uncertainty in the assessment of benefits and risks to FDA stakeholders.

11:20 a.m. Background and Session Objectives (*5 min.*)

ROBERT RATNER, *Workshop Co-Chair*
Chief Scientific and Medical Officer
American Diabetes Association

11:25 a.m. **Overview of Risk Communication** (*15 min.*)

BARUCH FISCHHOFF, *Workshop Co-Chair*
Howard Heinz University Professor
Department of Social and Decision Sciences
Department of Engineering and Public Policy
Carnegie Mellon University

11:40 a.m. **Risk Communication in the Context of Pharmaceuticals** (*15 min.*)

LISA M. SCHWARTZ
Professor, Departments of Medicine and Community & Family Medicine
Dartmouth Medical School
Co-Director, Medicine in the Media Program
The Dartmouth Institute for Health Policy and Clinical Practice

STEVEN WOLOSHIN
Professor, Departments of Medicine and Community & Family Medicine
Dartmouth Medical School
Co-Director, Medicine in the Media Program
The Dartmouth Institute for Health Policy and Clinical Practice

11:55 a.m. **What Are the Sources of Uncertainty When a Patient Is Faced with Choice?** (*15 min.*)

KIMBERLY MCCLEARY
Director of Strategic Initiatives
FasterCures

12:10 p.m. **LUNCH** (*40 min.*)

12:50 p.m. **Reintroducing the Tysabri Case Study** (*15 min.*)

ROBERT TEMPLE
Deputy Director for Clinical Science
Acting Deputy Director, Office of Drug Evaluation I
Center for Drug Evaluation and Research
U.S. Food and Drug Administration

1:05 p.m. **Media Analysis: Tysabri Case Study** (*20 min.*)

LISA M. SCHWARTZ
Professor, Departments of Medicine and Community & Family Medicine
Dartmouth Medical School
Co-Director, Medicine in the Media Program
The Dartmouth Institute for Health Policy and Clinical Practice

STEVEN WOLOSHIN
Professor, Departments of Medicine and Community & Family Medicine
Dartmouth Medical School
Co-Director, Medicine in the Media Program
The Dartmouth Institute for Health Policy and Clinical Practice

1:25 p.m. **Discussion on Communicating Uncertainty in Benefit and Risk Assessments of Pharmaceutical Products: Tysabri and Beyond** (*60 min.*)

Session III Speakers and:

CARMEN BOZIC
Senior Vice President
Clinical and Safety Sciences
Biogen Idec

ROBERT FOX
Staff Neurologist
Mellen Center for Multiple Sclerosis
Cleveland Clinic

Alice Hughes
Deputy Director for Safety of the Division of Neurology
Center for Drug Evaluation and Research
U.S. Food and Drug Administration

Joyce Korvick
Deputy Director for Safety, Division of Gastroenterology and Inborn Error Products
Office of Drug Evaluation III
Center for Drug Evaluation and Research
U.S. Food and Drug Administration

Cynthia Sitcov
Patient Representative & Voting Member
U.S. Food and Drug Administration, Central and Peripheral Systems Advisory Committee, 2005–Present

Discussion Moderator: Gavin Huntley-Fenner, Human Factors and Safety Consultant, Huntley-Fenner Advisors

2:25 p.m. **BREAK** (*15 min.*)

2:40 p.m. **Public Comment Period** (*30 min.*)

SESSION IV: CONCLUDING DISCUSSION: LESSONS LEARNED AND POTENTIAL STRATEGIES FOR A WAY FORWARD

Session Objectives:

- Discuss key themes from the workshop series.
  - What are key techniques and approaches for identifying, characterizing, and addressing uncertainty?
  - How do we communicate uncertainty in evidence regarding benefit–risk assessment?
- Describe key gaps in understanding and explore how best to address those gaps.
- Highlight potential pivotal opportunities to advance more systematic and structured approaches to characterizing and communicating the sources of uncertainty in the assessment of benefits and risks.
  - How do we shape an agenda for next steps to address these issues?

3:10 p.m. **Reflections from the Workshop Co-Chairs** (*10 min.*)

Baruch Fischhoff, *Workshop Co-Chair*
Howard Heinz University Professor
Department of Social and Decision Sciences
Department of Engineering and Public Policy
Carnegie Mellon University

Robert Ratner, *Workshop Co-Chair*
Chief Scientific and Medical Officer
American Diabetes Association

3:20 p.m. **Brainstorming Discussion of Key Themes from the Workshop Series** (*80 min.*)

3:20 p.m. **Segment One: Identifying and Mitigating Uncertainty Through Maximizing the Value of Evidence**

Reflections from Discussion Lead

Discussion Lead: Robert Temple, U.S. Food and Drug Administration (*5 min.*)

3:25 p.m. Discussion with Workshop Participants (*15 min.*)

3:40 p.m. **Segment Two: Characterizing and Understanding Uncertainties**

Reflections from Discussion Lead

Discussion Lead: Paul Seligman, Amgen Inc. (*5 min.*)

3:45 p.m. Discussion with Workshop Participants (*15 min.*)

4:00 p.m. **Segment Three: Eliciting Values from Stakeholders, Particularly Patients**

Reflections from Discussion Lead

Discussion Lead: Kimberly McCleary, *FasterCures* (*5 min.*)

4:05 p.m. Discussion with Workshop Participants (*15 min.*)

4:20 p.m. **Segment Four: Communicating Uncertainty About Benefit and Risk Assessments of Pharmaceutical Products**

Reflections from Discussion Lead

Discussion Lead: Gavin Huntley-Fenner, Huntley-Fenner Advisors (*5 min.*)

4:25 p.m. Discussion with Workshop Participants (*15 min.*)

4:40 p.m. **Reflecting on Tactics and Strategies for a Way Forward** (*20 min.*)

Discussion Moderators: Workshop Co-Chairs, Baruch Fischhoff, Carnegie Mellon University; and Robert Ratner, American Diabetes Association

5:00 p.m. Adjourn

Appendix B

FDA Case Studies[1]

Tysabri and the Risk of Progressive Multifocal Leukoencephalopathy (PML)[2]

SUMMARY

In February 2005, four months after its initial approval to treat patients with multiple sclerosis, Tysabri was withdrawn from the market because of concern about the risk of a life-threatening, frequently fatal, brain infection, PML. At the time, there was considerable uncertainty about the magnitude of the risk of PML to patients exposed to Tysabri and whether there were any identifiable risk factors that could be reliably used to identify patients at greater risk. In making its decision on whether to allow re-marketing of the drug, FDA considered whether the risk of PML (and uncertainty about the risk) outweighed the drug's recognized substantial benefit.

[1] Case studies were developed by FDA staff to inform the discussions at the IOM workshops. Text is reproduced here as originally submitted.

[2] Version Date: February 10, 2014. This summary was developed for purposes of discussion at the February 12–13, 2014, IOM/FDA Public Workshop: Characterizing and Communicating Uncertainty in the Assessment of Benefits and Risks.

INTRODUCTION[3]

Tysabri (natalizumab) was originally approved in 2004 for relapsing forms of multiple sclerosis (MS), a progressively debilitating neurological disease. There is no known cure for MS and the disease frequently progresses to severe disability and/or death. Approximately 400,000 individuals currently live with MS in the U.S.[4]

Tysabri represented a novel treatment mechanism for MS, believed to work by interfering with the movement of inflammatory white blood cells from the blood vessels into the brain and spinal cord. It is administered through intravenous infusion, typically on a monthly basis. Other effective treatments such as interferons and Copaxone (glatiramer acetate) were available at the time, but a substantial number of patients with relapsing MS remained untreated for many reasons, including lack of efficacy or tolerability of existing treatments. Tysabri appeared to be substantially more effective, with a significantly greater reduction in relapse rates over these treatments.

Previously-approved drugs had required clinical trials showing evidence of benefit through two years. The results of Tysabri were so promising in the first year that the drug was granted an accelerated approval[5] on the basis of 1-year interim results of the clinical trials. At the time of approval, Tysabri's safety profile was acceptable given the demonstrated benefits.

In February 2005, four months after approval, the sponsor notified FDA of two cases of PML, a rare, frequently fatal viral infection in the brain. Both cases occurred in patients receiving Tysabri for MS. In light of this, the sponsor voluntarily withdrew Tysabri from the market and suspended all clinical trials. By that time, about 7,000 patients had received at least one dose of Tysabri.

In September 2005, after conducting an extensive safety assessment, the sponsor submitted additional efficacy and safety evidence and requested reauthorization to market the drug. FDA's re-marketing decision hinged in large part on its conclusions about the risk of PML associated with Tysabri.

---

[3] In addition to the links embedded in the summary text, for relevant material from FDA on this topic see http://www.fda.gov/Drugs/DrugSafety/PostmarketDrugSafetyInformationforPatientsandProviders/ucm107198.htm (accessed August 23, 2014).

[4] Figure reported by the National Multiple Sclerosis Society, see http://www.nationalmssociety.org/about-the-society/ms-prevalence/index.aspx (accessed August 23, 2014).

[5] Federal regulations (21 CFR 601 subpart E) allow accelerated approval of new biologic therapies that provide meaningful benefit over existing treatments for serious or life-threatening illnesses. As a condition of the accelerated approval, the sponsor was required to verify that the demonstrated clinical benefit and safety was sustained in the second year.

In its review, FDA considered the following questions:

- What is the magnitude of risk of PML to patients exposed to Tysabri?
- Are there identifiable factors that can be used to screen for patients at higher risk for PML or otherwise mitigate the risk of PML?

ASSESSING THE RISK OF PML (BASED ON AVAILABLE EVIDENCE IN 2006)

The sponsor's safety assessment included a comprehensive clinical and neurological evaluation of the clinical trial subjects who had been exposed to Tysabri. FDA determined that the design, implementation, and analysis of the safety assessment were adequate. The assessment confirmed the two previously-identified PML cases but did not identify any other cases, out of 1869 MS patients treated for a median duration of 120 weeks. An additional case, however, was identified in a patient with Crohn's disease (the sponsor had also been assessing the drug for treatment of this gastrointestinal disease). In total, 3 cases were identified in a population of ~3,000 patients exposed in the clinical trials.[6]

Below are some of the additional factors pertinent to FDA's 2006 assessment of the risk of PML:

- PML is extremely rare in the general population. The death rate associated with PML in the U.S. in 2002-2005 was 0.66/1,000,000.[7] The disease typically affects individuals with suppressed immune systems. PML had not previously been associated with MS.
- Tysabri's mechanism of action raised a theoretical concern about an increase in risk of infections. In the clinical trials, the overall risk of infections (serious and non-serious) was similar for Tysabri vs. placebo. However, the drug appeared to cause an increased rate of specific types of serious atypical and opportunistic infections, including viral meningitis, herpes infections, pulmonary infections, gastrointestinal infections, and, of course, PML.
- Both MS PML cases were patients who took Tysabri in conjunction with an immunomodulating interferon drug, Avonex. However, use of interferons alone had not been associated with PML. The

[6] A report of the sponsor's safety assessment, published in 2006, reported a 95 percent confidence interval of 0.2/1000–2.8/1000. See Yousry, T.A., et al. 2006. Evaluation of patients treated with natalizumab for progressive multifocal leukoencephalopathy. *N Engl J Med* 354(9):924-933.

[7] Christensen, K. L., et al. 2010. Progressive multifocal leukoencephalopathy deaths in the USA, 1979-2005. *Neuroepidemiology* 35(3):178-184.

Crohn's patient also had a significant history of immunosuppressive use.

- PML is thought to be caused by the John Cunningham virus (JCV), which is carried in a dormant state by many people. At the time, there was no reliable test to detect JCV exposure.
- Diagnosis of PML requires clinical, neuroimaging, and virologic evidence. Early diagnosis of PML in MS patients can be particularly challenging because the signs and symptoms of PML are similar to those of MS.
- The majority of patients in the MS trials were enrolled for ≥2 years. Both MS PML cases occurred after approximately 2 years of exposure. However few patients in the development program had been exposed for 3+ years, resulting in uncertainty of the effect of longer-term exposure on the magnitude of the PML risk.
- In 2005, there was no known effective treatment for PML.

IMPACT OF UNCERTAINTY ON FDA'S DECISION-MAKING

The submitted additional evidence increased FDA's confidence that the PML cases were caused by Tysabri and that the overall risk of PML was on the order of 1 in 1,000 patients. However, the assessment did little to resolve uncertainty about whether the risk was related to any underlying factors, particularly concomitant use of immunosuppressing drugs, JCV exposure, and duration of Tysabri use. No other new serious safety concerns were identified in FDA's review to re-market Tysabri. Further, the additional efficacy evidence submitted in response to the accelerated approval requirement (the results of the 2-year study) strengthened FDA's assessment of the drug's benefit. Therefore, the question FDA faced was whether the risk of PML (and residual uncertainty about that risk) outweighed the substantial benefit of the drug to MS patients.

In March 2006, FDA convened an advisory committee (AC) meeting to gather expert input into the Agency's decision. At the meeting, patients, family, and health care providers testified to the difference that Tysabri had made in the lives of MS patients, as well as the willingness of patients to continue treatment despite the risk of PML. The AC members voted unanimously to reintroduce Tysabri to the market. However, they voted unanimously that the drug should be restricted to use: (a) as monotherapy (i.e., not to be used in combination with other MS drugs), and (b) in patients with relapsing forms of MS. They were divided, however, on whether the drug should be limited to use only as a second-line therapy (i.e., only in patients who have not responded adequately to or are intolerant of other treatments).

FDA concurred with the 2006 AC recommendations. As FDA concluded in its 2006 decision memo,[8] "in the face of these potential risks, the benefit of treatment with Tysabri clearly justifies its re-introduction into the market [with certain requirements] . . . and that physicians and patients should be given the opportunity to decide if this treatment is appropriate in any given case." The Agency remained concerned, however, about the inability to (a) identify individual patients who are at greater risk of contracting PML, and (b) to mitigate death or other serious effects of PML. FDA cautioned that "if marketing is permitted, we fully expect that additional cases of PML, many likely to be fatal, will occur . . . and it is a fact that patients, their families, and prescribers will need to consider very seriously."[9]

Thus, in June 2006, Tysabri was allowed back on the market, with a number of requirements:

1. The indication was restricted to use as monotherapy and only in patients with relapsing forms of the disease. Labeling further recommended use as a second-line treatment.
2. A boxed warning and detailed safety information on PML, including what was known and not known about the risk, was included in the revised (2006) product labeling.[10]
3. The risk management plan included a restricted distribution program (called TOUCH) requiring prescribing and administration only by certified health care providers, use only in patients enrolled in the program and who met necessary conditions, documented patient counselling, and patient evaluation at 3 and 6 months after initial treatment and every 6 months thereafter.
4. A prospective, observational post-marketing safety study (called TYGRIS) was required, enrolling 5,000 patients followed for 5 years to monitor for safety concerns, including PML and other serious infections.

SINCE THE 2006 RE-MARKET AUTHORIZATION

Tysabri was approved for the Crohn's disease indication in January 2008. At that time, no new PML cases had been reported in either the post-

---

[8] See http://www.accessdata.fda.gov/drugsatfda_docs/label/2006/125104Orig1s015SumR.pdf (accessed August 23, 2014).

[9] Opening remarks by Dr. Russell Katz, Director of the Division of Neurology Products, at the 2006 FDA Advisory Committee Meeting on the subject of Tysabri remarketing. http://www.fda.gov/ohrms/dockets/ac/06/transcripts/2006-4208T1.pdf (accessed August 23, 2014).

[10] For more information see http://www.accessdata.fda.gov/drugsatfda_docs/label/2006/125104s015LBL.pdf (accessed August 23, 2014).

market setting or in the sponsor's drug development program. However, there remained uncertainty about factors that contributed to the risk of PML. Similar to the MS indication, the Crohn's indication was limited to use as a second-line therapy and only for patients with moderate to severe symptoms. It also required restricted distribution through the TOUCH program.

The first two post-market cases of PML since the drug's 2006 re-marketing were reported to FDA in the summer of 2008. At that time, ~39,000 patients had received treatment with Tysabri worldwide, with ~12,000 patients having been treated for at least one year. Both cases occurred in MS patients in Europe, and both patients were receiving Tysabri as monotherapy. However, FDA concluded in an August 2008 advisory[11] that it "still believes that Tysabri monotherapy may confer a lower risk of PML than when Tysabri is used together with other immunomodulatory medications."

Today, the risk of PML associated with Tysabri is much better understood. As of September 3, 2013, 401 cases of PML had been reported worldwide. Table 1 presents the stratified risk estimates for the U.S. population, showing how the risk depends on length of exposure, presence of anti-JVC antibodies, and immunosuppressant use. The current product labeling[12] recommends considering these factors in the context of expected benefit when initiating and continuing treatment. Additionally, an anti-JCV antibody detection test was cleared[13] by FDA in January 2012.

Table 1. Estimated United States Incidence of PML Stratified by Risk Factor

Anti-JVC Antibody Negative	TYSABRI Exposure	Anti-JVC Antibody Positive	
		No Prior Use of Immunosuppressant	Prior Use of Immunosuppressant
<1/1,000	1–24 months	<1/1,000	1/1,000
	25–48 months	3/1,000	13/1,000
	49–72 months	7/1,000	9/1,000

The experience with Tysabri has also heightened FDA's awareness and consideration of potential drug-induced PML risk. For example, a

[11] For more information see http://www.fda.gov/Drugs/DrugSafety/PostmarketDrugSafetyInformationforPatientsandProviders/ucm126592.htm (accessed August 23, 2014).

[12] For more information see http://www.accessdata.fda.gov/drugsatfda_docs/label/2013/125104s840s847s889lbl.pdf (accessed August 23, 2014).

[13] For more information see http://www.fda.gov/NewsEvents/Newsroom/PressAnnouncements/ucm288471.htm (accessed August 23, 2014).

central question in a 2013 AC meeting on vedolizumab, another drug indicated for Crohn's disease with a similar mechanism of action, was whether the applicant had adequately characterized the potential risk of PML.[14]

FDA'S COMMUNICATIONS ABOUT PML[15]

FDA first issued a public health advisory[16] on Feb. 28, 2005, announcing the first two PML cases and Tysabri's market withdrawal. FDA issued a press release[17] at the time re-marketing was approved, which outlined the narrower indication and the TOUCH program. In addition to the 2008 advisory[18] described above, FDA has issued three Drug Safety Communications: Feb. 5, 2010,[19] confirming that PML risk increases with the number of Tysabri infusions received; April 22, 2011,[20] confirming that PML risk is increased in patients who have taken other drugs that suppress the immune system; and Jan. 20, 2012,[21] confirming that PML risk is increased in people who test positive for JVC.

---

[14] For more information see FDA's background document for the December 9, 2013, Advisory Committee meeting on the subject of vedolizumab: http://www.fda.gov/downloads/AdvisoryCommittees/CommitteesMeetingMaterials/Drugs/GastrointestinalDrugsAdvisoryCommittee/UCM377618.pdf (accessed August 23, 2014).

[15] See http://www.fda.gov/Drugs/DrugSafety/PostmarketDrugSafetyInformationforPatientsandProviders/ucm107198.htm (accessed August 23, 2014) for all communications.

[16] See http://www.fda.gov/NewsEvents/Newsroom/PressAnnouncements/2005/ucm108413.htm (accessed August 23, 2014).

[17] See http://www.fda.gov/NewsEvents/Newsroom/PressAnnouncements/2006/ucm108662.htm (accessed August 23, 2014).

[18] See http://www.fda.gov/Drugs/DrugSafety/PostmarketDrugSafetyInformationforPatientsandProviders/ucm126592.htm (accessed August 23, 2014).

[19] See http://www.fda.gov/Drugs/DrugSafety/PostmarketDrugSafetyInformationforPatientsandProviders/ucm199872.htm (accessed August 23, 2014).

[20] See http://www.fda.gov/Drugs/DrugSafety/ucm252045.htm (accessed August 23, 2014).

[21] See http://www.fda.gov/Drugs/DrugSafety/ucm288186.htm (accessed August 23, 2014).

Uncertainty About CV Risk Associated with LAMA Drugs for COPD[22]

SUMMARY

In December 2013, FDA approved a novel combination product, Anoro Ellipta, as a long-term maintenance treatment for patients with chronic obstructive pulmonary disease (COPD). One of its agents, umeclidinium, is a member of a class of long-acting antimuscarinic agents (LAMAs), which has been the subject of concern since 2007, when pooled analyses suggested an increased risk of stroke, cardiovascular death, and myocardial infarction (MI) associated with tiotropium, one drug in this class. Since that time, various meta-analyses and randomized clinical trials have drawn conflicting conclusions about the cardiovascular (CV) risk of inhaled antimuscarinic agents, and this uncertainty has influenced FDA's decision-making regarding other drugs in the class. The low numbers of major adverse cardiac events (MACE) observed in the Anoro Ellipta pre-market clinical trials made it difficult to draw definitive conclusions about CV risk for this specific product. Therefore, an important question in the Anoro Ellipta approval decision was whether to require a post-market study to further assess potential CV risk. This case highlights the impact uncertainty can have on decisions regarding a class of drugs, as well as the issues presented by conflicting evidence from multiple sources.

INTRODUCTION

In December 2013, FDA approved Anoro Ellipta (umeclidinium and vilanterol inhalation powder) as a long-term maintenance treatment for patients with chronic obstructive pulmonary disease (COPD). COPD refers to a group of progressive, debilitating respiratory conditions, including emphysema and chronic bronchitis. It is the third leading cause of death in the U.S. There are several pharmaceutical options to treat COPD, including inhaled bronchodilators and steroids. The approved dose for Anoro Ellipta is one inhalation (umeclidinium/vilanterol 62.5 mcg/25 mcg) once daily.

Anoro Ellipta is a combination bronchodilator inhalation product, with two active ingredients. Umeclidinium is a long-acting antimuscarinic agent (LAMA) and vilanterol is a long-acting beta2-adrenergic agonist

[22] Version Date: February 5, 2014. This summary was developed for purposes of discussion at the February 12–13, 2014 IOM/FD, Public Workshop: Characterizing and Communicating Uncertainty in the Assessment of Benefits and Risks.

(LABA). Neither component is currently approved in the U.S. as a single-ingredient product; however, vilanterol is available as part of a related combination product, Breo Ellipta (fluticasone furoate and vilanterol inhalation powder).

The development program for Anoro Ellipta included 8,138 patients with COPD in four 6-month trials, one 12-month long-term safety trial, and 9 trials of shorter duration. Over 2,400 COPD patients were treated with either the 62.5 mcg/25 mcg umeclidinium/vilanterol combination or a higher dose of the combination (125 mcg/25 mcg umeclidinium/vilanterol). The product showed improved bronchodilation over placebo and over either individual component. A major safety concern for Anoro Ellipta, as for the class of LABAs, is an increased risk of asthma-related death, and the approved product labeling[23] includes a boxed warning highlighting this risk.

This case study focuses on another potential safety concern identified by FDA in its review of Anoro Ellipta. LAMAs have been the subject of concern since 2007, when a pooled analysis of controlled clinical trial data suggested an increased risk of stroke, cardiovascular death, and myocardial infarction (MI) associated with tiotropium, one drug in this class. Since that time, various meta-analyses and randomized clinical trials have drawn conflicting conclusions about the cardiovascular (CV) risk of inhaled antimuscarinic agents. This uncertainty has influenced FDA's decision-making regarding other drugs in this class (described below).

The low numbers of major adverse cardiac events (MACE) observed in the Anoro Ellipta pre-market clinical trials made it difficult to draw definitive conclusions about CV risk of this product. Therefore, an important question in FDA's approval decision for Anoro Ellipta was whether to require a post-market study to further assess potential CV risk. As FDA explained in the Anoro Ellipta decision memo[24] (p. 13):

> [T]he question becomes at what point we feel that a hypothesized safety issue caused by a class of drugs has been answered and further exploration is not necessary? Put another way, when a concern is discovered by meta-analysis, when is there enough data from randomized trials to assuage this concern?

[23] See http://www.accessdata.fda.gov/drugsatfda_docs/label/2013/203975s000lbl.pdf (accessed August 23, 2014).

[24] See http://www.accessdata.fda.gov/drugsatfda_docs/nda/2013/203975Orig1s000OD Memo.pdf (accessed August 23, 2014).

A LOOK AT THE PAST: ASSESSING CV RISK FOR OTHER LAMAS

Understanding FDA's decision-making in the Anoro Ellipta case requires a look at how uncertainty was addressed in previous LAMA cases.

Tiotropium–Spiriva HandiHaler

Spiriva (tiotropium), delivered by the HandiHaler device, was the first LAMA to be approved by FDA, in 2004. At the time of approval, the available safety data raised the possibility of increased risk of "heart rate and rhythm disorders," but risk of major CV events was not a major concern. The first indication of a possible CV risk associated with tiotropium was reported to FDA in 2007 by the drug's sponsor. Results of a separate meta-analysis (Singh 2008)[25] showed an increased relative risk of CV events with tiotropium and another short-acting antimuscarinic agent over control (RR 1.60 (95% CI (1.22-2.10)). However, subsequent results[26] of a large (~6,000 patients), 4-year, randomized, controlled trial (called UPLIFT), did not show an increase in CV events associated with tiotropium, contradicting the meta-analysis results.

FDA conducted a comprehensive review to evaluate the strength of the 2007 pooled analysis, the 2008 meta-analysis, and the UPLIFT clinical trial. It identified a number of methodological limitations of the pooled and meta-analyses including potential study selection bias and potential differences in patient characteristics in treatment arms (e.g., sicker patients on placebo may have dropped out more). FDA's assessment and conclusion on the CV risk of Spiriva HandiHaler is explained in a *New England Journal of Medicine* (*NEJM*) Perspectives article.[27] There, FDA stated (p. 1099):

> Because of the strength of the UPLIFT data, the absence of a strong signal related to stroke or cardiovascular events with tiotropium, and the potential methodologic limitations of the Singh meta-analysis, the FDA concluded that current data do not support the conclusion that there is an increased risk of stroke, heart attack, or death associated with tiotropium HandiHaler.

---

[25] Singh, S., Y. K. Loke, and C. D. Furberg 2008. *JAMA* 300:1439-1450. [Erratum, 2009. *JAMA* 301:1227-1230.]

[26] Tashkin, D. P., B. Celli, S. Senn, et al. 2008. *N Engl J Med* 359:1543-1554.

[27] Michele, T. M., et al. 2010. *N Engl J Med* 363:1097-1099.

Tiotropium–Spiriva Respimat

At the same time the Spiriva HandiHaler CV risk signal was being assessed, FDA was also reviewing for market approval another tiotropium product, Spiriva Respimat, which had a different formulation and delivery device. In this case, three pre-market clinical trials showed an imbalance of deaths, of varying causes, including cardiac failure and MI, between the drug and placebo. Further, because the delivery of locally-acting drugs like inhaled bronchodilators differ depending on their formulation and device, FDA was unable to draw clear conclusions about the safety of Spiriva Respimat on the basis of the available evidence for Spiriva HandiHaler (and vice versa). Spiriva Respimat is not approved for marketing in the U.S., although the drug is approved elsewhere.

Subsequently, the drug's sponsor conducted a large (>17,000 patients), prospective safety trial (TIOSPIR) to better assess the safety of Spiriva Respimat compared to Spiriva HandiHaler. The TIOSPIR results were published in October 2013[28] and indicate that the risk of death and of major cardiovascular adverse events is similar for the two tiotropium products. While the TIOSPIR results appear to be reassuring, it should be noted that the data from this trial have not yet been submitted to FDA for review.

Tudorza Pressair

Tudorza Pressair (aclidinium bromide inhalation powder) was approved in 2012. The pre-market evidence included a safety database limited in size, which hindered FDA's ability to draw definitive conclusions.[29] Because of this, and given the lingering uncertainty of possible disparate safety profiles of tiotropium delivered by different devices (the TIOSPIR trial was not yet published), a post-market CV outcome trial was required as a condition of the drug's approval. In the Anoro Ellipta decision memo[30] (p. 13), Dr. Curtis Rosebraugh explained the thinking about aclidinium at that time: "At the time of the review for aclidinium, I did not believe we had enough data to exonerate tiotropium, thereby casting a shadow on the LAMA class."

---

[28] Wise, R. A., et al. 2013. *N Engl J Med* 369:1491-1501.

[29] The safety database included 733 patients exposed to the proposed 400 mcg dose of aclidinium for approximately 6 months, and 329 patients for approximately 1 year. It is important to note that these numbers do not represent unique patients; that is, the 329 patients listed as having an exposure for 1 year are also included among the 733 patients listed as having an exposure for 6 months.

[30] See http://www.accessdata.fda.gov/drugsatfda_docs/nda/2013/203975Orig1s000OD Memo.pdf (accessed August 23, 2014).

ASSESSMENT OF THE SUBMITTED EVIDENCE FOR ANORO ELLIPTA

In its review of Anoro Ellipta, FDA conducted a comprehensive evaluation of the pre-market data submitted by the drug's sponsor to support approval. However, there were limitations that hindered FDA's ability to draw conclusions with respect to Anoro Ellipta's CV safety profile. Like most pre-market clinical trials, the Anoro Ellipta trials were not designed (e.g., in terms of size or duration) to conclusively assess CV risk. In addition, the Anoro Ellipta program was also hampered by another issue common to clinical trials, namely, the generalizability of data gathered on a specific patient population in a highly controlled setting to the broader COPD population in the "real-world." The limitations of the pre-market data are highlighted in the Anoro Ellipta decision memo,[31] which states (p.9) that "any results are fragile at best and conclusion would be tenuous. The most that can be said is that there is not a consistent trend of MACE events indicating harm with drug use compared to placebo (or dose-response increase)."

IMPACT OF UNCERTAINTY ON FDA'S DECISION-MAKING FOR ANORO ELLIPTA

FDA concluded that substantial evidence of efficacy and overall safety had been demonstrated and that the benefits outweighed the risks of Anoro Ellipta. However, the question remained whether additional post-market studies would be required to further assess CV safety for this drug.

The drug sponsor had proposed conducting observational studies to explore any possible CV risks. However, at this time, FDA does not generally consider observational studies to be adequate to quantitatively answer questions regarding a drug's potential to cause increased CV events. Therefore, if additional evidence was necessary, it would have to be in the form of a large, randomized clinical trial.

After considering the totality of evidence, FDA concluded that a post-market CV clinical trial was not necessary. In the Anoro Ellipta decision memo[32] (p. 13), Dr. Rosebraugh explained:

> [If the published results for TIOSPIR withstand FDA scrutiny], it would seem that the realization needs to be made that the advice for outcome trials for LAMA agents was based on a meta-analysis for tiotropium/

[31] See http://www.accessdata.fda.gov/drugsatfda_docs/nda/2013/203975Orig1s000ODMemo.pdf (accessed August 23, 2014).

[32] See http://www.accessdata.fda.gov/drugsatfda_docs/nda/2013/203975Orig1s000ODMemo.pdf (accessed August 23, 2014).

ipratropium (and possible concerns of class effects), which has proven to be a false signal. If this is a logical progression of thought, then contemplation must occur regarding at what point CV outcome trials should no longer be required of LAMA agents. I believe we are at that point.

BROADER RELEVANCE TO FDA'S CONSIDERATION OF UNCERTAINTY

This case highlights the impact uncertainty can have on decisions regarding a class of drugs, as well as the issues surrounding the uncertainty presented by conflicting evidence from multiple sources. These issues are not isolated to this class of drugs. For example, both issues are important in cases concerning the assessment of CV risk in Avandia (rosiglitazone) and other drugs to treat Type-2 diabetes mellitus.[33]

This case also highlights a challenge in determining the role of meta-analysis in FDA's assessment of benefits and risks of drugs. FDA considers meta-analysis to be an important tool for safety assessment in the regulation of pharmaceutical products.[34] However, meta-analyses present challenges in their design, evaluation, and interpretation. For example, in its 2010 NEJM article (p. 1099),[35] FDA commented:

We have entered an era of increasingly frequent publication of meta-analyses, some of which identify potential safety signals. Such publication commonly leads to urgent calls to take immediate regulatory action, without acknowledgment of potential pitfalls in the interpretation of data from meta-analyses and pooled analyses, such as those encountered in the tiotropium evaluation. We must use measured restraint during our evaluations to ensure that safe drugs remain on the market and that their use is not restricted in a way that unnecessarily denies beneficial interventions to patients who need them.

FDA'S COMMUNICATIONS TO THE PUBLIC

FDA's communications on this topic have primarily focused on the potential CV risk in tiotropium.[36] In March, 2008, FDA issued an Early

[33] The comparison of rosiglitazone to the case of LAMAs is discussed in the Anoro Ellipta decision memo.

[34] Given its importance, FDA recently conducted a public workshop on the topic of meta-analysis. See http://www.fda.gov/ForIndustry/UserFees/PrescriptionDrugUserFee/ucm360080.htm (accessed August 23, 2014).

[35] Michele, T. M., et al. 2010. *N Engl J Med* 363:1097-1099.

[36] FDA's communications on tiotropium are available at http://www.fda.gov/Drugs/DrugSafety/PostmarketDrugSafetyInformationforPatientsandProviders/ucm107272.htm (accessed August 23, 2014).

Communication (now archived[37]), which notified the public of the sponsor's pooled analysis first suggesting an association between Spiriva HandiHaler and stroke. FDA updated this communication in October, 2008, announcing the publication of the Singh 2008 meta-analysis and the completion of the clinical trial UPLIFT. In 2010, in addition to its NEJM article, FDA posted on its website another update[38] explaining its conclusions that the available data do not support an association between Spiriva HandiHaler and CV risk.

---

[37] See http://www.fda.gov/Drugs/DrugSafety/PostmarketDrugSafetyInformationforPatientsandProviders/DrugSafetyInformationforHeathcareProfessionals/ucm070651.htm (accessed August 23, 2014).

[38] See http://www.fda.gov/Drugs/DrugSafety/PostmarketDrugSafetyInformationforPatientsandProviders/DrugSafetyInformationforHeathcareProfessionals/ucm197429.htm (accessed August 23, 2014).

Appendix C

Bibliography[1]

CHAPTER 2: IDENTIFYING AND CHARACTERIZING UNCERTAINTY

Workshop presentation by Tarek A. Hammad: Key Sources of Uncertainty in the Assessment of Benefits and Risks of Pharmaceuticals and Associated Challenges

Berlin, J. A., B. J. Crowe, E. Whalen, H. A. Xia, C. E. Koro, and J. Kuebler. 2012. Meta-analysis of clinical trial safety data in a drug development program: Answers to frequently asked questions. *Clinical Trials* 10:20-31.

Eichler, H. G., B. Bloechl-Daum, D. Brasseur, A. Breckenridge, H. Leufkens, J. Raine, T. Salmonson, C. K. Schneider, and G. Rasi. 2013. The risks of risk aversion in drug regulation. *Nature Reviews Drug Discovery* 12(12):907-916.

Hammad, T. A., G. A. Neyarapally, S. Iyasu, J. A. Staffa, and G. Dal Pan. 2013. The future of population-based postmarket drug risk assessment: A regulator's perspective. *Clinical Pharmacology & Therapeutics* 94(3):349-358.

Maro, J. C., and J. S. Brown. 2011. Impact of exposure accrual on sequential postmarket evaluations: A simulation study. *Pharmacoepidemiology and Drug Safety* (20):1184-1191.

[1] This bibliography contains resources provided during presentations by workshop speakers but not necessarily cited in the workshop summary report. These resources are included here as additional direction for readers interested in further exploration of the topics discussed at the workshop.

Workshop presentation by Deborah A. Zarin: ClinicalTrials.gov and Addressing Challenges in Finding Evidence

Earley, A., J. Lau, and K. Uhlig. 2012. Haphazard reporting of deaths in clinical trials: A review of cases of ClinicalTrials.gov records and matched publications: A cross-sectional study. http://bmjopen.bmj.com/content/3/1/e001963.full.pdf+html (accessed September 13, 2014).

Jüni, P., A. W. S. Rutjes, and P. A. Dieppe. 2002. Are selective COX 2 inhibitors superior to traditional non-steroidal anti-inflammatory drugs? *British Medical Journal* 324:1287-1288. http://www.bmj.com/content/324/7349/1287.full.pdf+html (accessed September 13, 2014).

Riveros, C., A. Deschartres, E. Perrodeau, R. Haneef, I. Boutron, and P. Ravaud. 2013. Timing and completeness of trial results posted at ClinicalTrials.gov and published in journals. *PLoS Medicine* 10(12):e1001566.

Ross, J. S., T. Tse, D. A. Zarin, H. Xu, L. Zhou, and H. M. Krumholz. 2012. Publication of NIH funded trials registered in ClinicalTrials.gov: Cross-sectional analysis. *British Medical Journal* 344:d7292.

Zarin, D. A., and T. Tse. 2013. Unambiguous identification of obesity trials. *New England Journal of Medicine* 368:580-581.

Zarin, D. A., T. Tse, R. J. Williams, R. M. Califf, and N. C. Ide. 2011. The ClinicalTrials.gov results database: Update and key issues. *New England Journal of Medicine* 364:852-860.

Workshop presentation by Michaela Kiernan: Identifying and Retaining Subgroups in Clinical Trials in the Context of Uncertainty About the External Validity of Clinical Trials

Goldberg, J. H., and M. Kiernan. 2005. Innovative techniques to address retention in a behavioral weight-loss trial. *Health Education Research* 20:439-447.

Kiernan, M., S. D. Brown, D. E. Schoffman, K. Lee, Katherine, A. C. King, C. B. Taylor, N. C. Schleicher, and M. G. Perri. 2013. Promoting healthy weight with "Stability Skills First": A randomized trial. *Journal of Consulting and Clinical Psychology* 81(2):336-346.

Moher, D., S. Hopewell, K. F. Schulz, V. Montori, P. C. Gøtzsche, P. J. Devereaux, D. Elbourne, M. Egger, and D. G. Altman. 2010. CONSORT 2010 Explanation and elaboration: Updated guidelines for reporting parallel group randomised trials. *British Medical Journal* 340:c869.

Workshop presentation by Sebastian Schneeweiss: Addressing Uncertainties in the Evaluation of Pharmaceutical Benefits and Harms During the Market Access Phase

Gagne, J. J., S. V. Wang, J. A. Rassen, and S. Schneeweiss. 2014. A modular, prospective, semi-automated drug safety monitoring system for use in a distributed data environment. *Pharmacoepidemiology and Drug Safety* 23:619-627.

Patrick, A. R., J. M. Franklin, M. C. Weinstein, R. J. Glynn, and S. Schneeweiss. 2013. Sequential value-of-information assessment for prospective drug safety monitoring using claims databases: The comparative safety of prasugrel v. clopidogrel. *Medical Decision Making* 33(7):949-960.

Schneeweiss, S., and J. Avorn. 2009. Antipsychotic agents and sudden cardiac death: How should we manage the risk? *New England Journal of Medicine* 360:294-296.

Workshop presentation by John P. A. Ioannidis: Systematic Approaches to Assessing the Internal and External Validity of Randomized Controlled Trials

Kappagoda, S., and J. P. A. Ioannidis. 2012. Neglected tropical diseases: Survey and geometry of randomised evidence. *British Medical Journal* 345:e6512.

Kim, D., J. Y. Tang, and J. P. A. Ioannidis. 2014. Network geometry shows evidence sequestration for medical vs. surgical practices: Treatments for basal cell carcinoma. *Journal of Clinical Epidemiology* 67(4):391-400.

Lathyris, D. N., N. A. Patsopoulos, G. Salanti, and J. P. A. Ioannidis. 2010. Industry sponsorship and selection of comparators in randomized clinical trials. *European Journal of Clinical Investigation* 40(2):172-182.

Mauri, D., N. P. Polyzos, G. Salanti, N. Pavlidis, and J. P. A. Ioannidis. 2008. Multiple-treatments meta-analysis of chemotherapy and targeted therapies in advanced breast cancer. *Journal of the National Cancer Institute* 100:1780-1791.

Mills, E. J., J. P. A. Ioannidis, and T. K. Schünemann. 2013. Demystifying trial networks and network meta-analysis. *British Medical Journal* 346:f2914.

Pereira, T. V., R. I. Horwitz, and J. P. A. Ioannidis. 2012. Empirical evaluation of very large treatment effects of medical interventions. *Journal of the American Medical Association* 308(16):1676-1684.

Salanti, G., S. Dias, N. J. Welton, A. E. Ades, V. Golfinopoulos, M. Kyrgiou, D. Mauri, and J. P. A. Ioannidis. 2010. Evaluating novel agent effects in multiple-treatments meta regression. *Statistics in Medicine* 29(23):2369-2383.

Saquib, N., J. Saquib, and J. P. A. Ioannidis. 2013. Practices and impact of primary outcome adjustment in randomized controlled trials: Meta-epidemiologic study. *British Medical Journal* 347:f4313.

Savovic, J., H. E. Jones, D. G. Altman, R. J. Harris, P. Jüni, J. Pildal, B. Als-Nielsen, E. M. Balk, C. Gluud, L. L. Gluud, J. P. A. Ioannidis, K. F. Schulz, R. Beynon, N. J. Welton, L. Wood, D. Moher, J. J. Deeks, and J. A. Sterne. 2012. Influence of reported study design characteristics on intervention effect estimates from randomized controlled trials. *Annals of Internal Medicine* 157(6):429-438.

Schulz, K. F., I. Chalmers, R. J. Hayes, and D. G. Altman. 1995. Empirical evidence of bias: Dimensions of methodological quality associated with estimates of treatment effects in controlled trials. *Journal of the American Medical Association* 273(5):408-413.

Siontis, K. C. M., E. Evangelou, and J. P. A. Ioannidis. 2011. Magnitude of effects in clinical trials published in high-impact general medical journals. *International Journal of Epidemiology* 40:1280-1291.

CHAPTER 3: THE REGULATORS' CHALLENGE

Workshop presentation by Mary H. Parks: Challenges to the Regulator in Communicating Uncertainties in Risks of Approved Pharmaceuticals

FDA (U.S. Food and Drug Administration). 2013. Structured approach to benefit–risk assessment in drug regulatory decision making, Draft PDUFA V implementation plan, February 2013, Fiscal Years 2013-2017. Washington, DC: FDA.

Workshop presentation by Robyn Lim: A Regulatory Approach to Uncertainty for the "Real World"

Hammond, J. S., R. L. Keeney, and H. Raiffa. 1999. *Smart choices. A practical guide to making better decisions*. Boston, MA: Harvard Business School Press.

Spiegelhalter, D. J. 2010. Quantifying and visualising uncertainty, presentation to Kings College, London, United Kingdom. http://www.mth.kcl.ac.uk/finmath/semfiles/DS.pdf (accessed September 13, 2014).

Workshop presentation by Theresa Mullin: FDA Patient-Focused Drug Development Initiative

FDA (U.S. Food and Drug Administration). 2013. *Structured approach to benefit–risk assessment in drug regulatory decision making, Draft PDUFA V implementation plan, February 2013, Fiscal Years 2013-2017*. Washington, DC: FDA.

CHAPTER 4: BASIC METHODOLOGIES AND APPLICATIONS FOR UNDERSTANDING AND EVALUATING UNCERTAINTY

Workshop presentation by M. Granger Morgan: Some Thoughts on Expert Elicitation

Evans, J. S. 1994. A distributional approach to characterizing low-dose cancer risk. *Risk Analysis* 14(1):25-34.

Evans, J. S., G. M. Gray, R. L. Sielken, A. E. Smith, C. Valdez-Flores, and J. D. Graham. 1994. Use of probabilistic expert judgment in uncertainty analysis of carcinogenic potency. *Regulatory Toxicology and Pharmacology* 20(1 Pt 1):15-36.

Henrion, M., and B. Fischhoff. 1986. Assessing uncertainty in physical constants. *American Journal of Physics* 54(9):791-798.

Morgan, M. G. 1998. Uncertainty analysis in risk assessment. *Human and Ecological Risk Assessment* 4(1):25-39.

Morgan, M. G. 2014. The use (and abuse) of expert elicitation in support of decision making for public policy. *Proceedings of the National Academy of Sciences of the United States of America* 111(20):7176-7184.

Morgan, M. G., M. Henrion, and M. Small. 1990. *Uncertainty: A guide to dealing with uncertainty in quantitative risk and policy analysis*. Cambridge, United Kingdom, and New York: Cambridge University Press.

Tversky, A., and D. Kahneman. 1974. Judgment under uncertainty: Heuristics and biases. *Science* 185(4157):1124-1131. Also: Kahneman, D., P. Slovic, and A. Tversky (Eds.). 1982. *Judgment under uncertainty: Heuristics and biases*. Cambridge, United Kingdom, and New York: Cambridge University Press.

Wallsten, T. S., D. V. Budescu, A. Rapoport, R. Zwick, and B. Forsyth. 1986. Measuring the vague meanings of probability terms. *Journal of Experimental Psychology: General* 155(4):348-365.

Workshop presentation by Joel Greenhouse: Bayesian Approaches to Evaluating Clinical Trial Data

Greenhouse, J. B., and H. Seltman. 2005. Using prior distributions to synthesize historical evidence: Comments on the Goodman-Sladky case study of IVIg in GBS. *Clinical Trials* 2(4):311-318.

Kass, R., and J. B. Greenhouse. 1989. Comment on "Investigating therapies of potentially great benefit: ECMO" by J. Ware. *Statistical Science* 4:31-37.

Spiegelhalter, D. J., K. R. Abrams, and J. P. Myles. 2004. Bayesian approaches to clinical trials and health care evaluation. Chichester, England: John Wiley & Sons.

Workshop presentation by David R. Mandel: Experiences in Implementing Uncertainty Assessments in the Defense/Intelligence Communities

Kent, S. 1964. *Words of estimative probability*. Reprinted in Steury (Ed.), Sherman Kent, and the Board of National Estimates. Washington, DC: Central Intelligence Agency, Center for the Study of Intelligence. https://www.cia.gov/library/center-for-the-study-of-intelligence/csi-publications/books-and-monographs/sherman-kent-and-the-board-of-national-estimates-collected-essays/6words.html (accessed August 14, 2014).

Kimmelman, J., J. Brehaut, D. Fergusson, A. J. London, D. Mandel, I. Shrier, and R. Steele. 2013-2016. Can researchers accurately predict trial outcomes? Work in progress, funded by Canadian Institutes of Health Research.

Mandel, D. R. 2007. *Toward a concept of risk for effective military decision making*. Defence Research and Development Canada, Toronto Technical Report 2007-124. Toronto, Canada: Defence Research and Development Canada. http://cradpdf.drdc-rddc.gc.ca/PDFS/unc68/p529014.pdf (accessed August 23, 2014).

Workshop presentation by Joseph Arvai: A Structured Approach to Risk–Benefit Assessment

Arvai, J., and L. Rivers III (Eds.). 2013. *Effective risk communication*. Brighton, United Kingdom: Routledge (Earthscan Risk in Society).

Fischhoff, B. 1982. *Judgment and decision making*. London, United Kingdom, and New York: Routledge (Earthscan Risk in Society).

Gregory, R., L. Failing, M. Harstone, G. Long, T. McDaniels, and D. Ohlson. 2012. *Structured decision making: A practical guide to environmental management choices.* Indianapolis, IN: Wiley-Blackwell.

Keeney, R. L. 1996. *Value-focused thinking: A path to creative decisionmaking.* Cambridge, MA: Harvard University Press.

NRC (National Research Council). 2003. *Understanding risk: Informing decisions in a democratic society.* Washington, DC: The National Academies Press.

Slovic, P. 2010. *The feeling of risk: New perspectives on risk perception.* Abingdon, Oxon, United Kingdom: Routledge (Earthscan Risk in Society).

Workshop presentation by Timothy McDaniels: Eliciting Values for Risk Management Choices: Principles and Approaches

FDA (U.S. Food and Drug Administration). 2009. *Guidance for industry: Format and content of proposed Risk Evaluation and Mitigation Strategies (REMS), REMS assessments, and proposed REMS modifications—Draft guidance.* http://www.fda.gov/downloads/Drugs/GuidanceComplianceRegulatoryInformation/Guidances/UCM184128.pdf (accessed August 14, 2014).

Workshop presentation by Charles F. Manski: Adaptive Partial Drug Approval

Eichler, H. G., K. Oye, L. G. Baird, E. Abadie, J. Brown, C. L. Drum, J. Ferguson, S. Garner, P. Honig, M. Hukkelhoven, J. C. W. Lim, R. Lim, M. M. Lumpkin, G. Neil, B. O'Rourke, E. Pezalla, D. Shoda, V. Seyfert-Margolis, E. V. Sigal, J. Sobotka, D. Tan, T. F. Unger, and G. Hirsch. 2012. Adaptive licensing: Taking the next step in the evolution of drug approval. *Clinical Pharmacology & Therapeutics* 91(3):426-437.

Manski, C. 2009. Diversified treatment under ambiguity. *International Economic Review* 50:1013-1041.

Manski, C. 2013. *Public policy in an uncertain world*. Boston, MA: Harvard University Press.

Tamura, R. N., D. E. Faries, J. S. Andersen, and J. H. Heiligenstein. 1994. A case study of an adaptive clinical trial in the treatment of out-patients with depressive disorder. *Journal of the American Statistical Association* 89:768-776.

CHAPTER 5: COMMUNICATING UNCERTAINTY

Workshop presentation by Baruch Fischhoff: Communicating Uncertainty

Bruine de Bruin, W., A. Parker, and B. Fischhoff. 2007. Individual differences in adult decision-making competence (A-DMC). *Journal of Personality and Social Psychology* 92:938-956.

Campbell, P. 2011. Understanding the receivers and the receptions of science's uncertain messages. *Philosophical Transactions of the Royal Society* 369:4891-4912.

Downs, J. S., W. Bruine de Bruin, and B. Fischhoff. 2008. Patients' vaccination comprehension and decisions. *Vaccine* 26:1595-1607.

Fischhoff, B. 1992. Giving advice: Decision theory perspectives on sexual assault. *American Psychologist* 47:577-588.

Fischhoff, B. 2011. Communicating the risks of terrorism (and anything else). *American Psychologist* 66:520-531.

Fischhoff, B. 2012. Communicating uncertainty: Fulfilling the duty to inform. *Issues in Science and Technology* 29:63-70.

Fischhoff, B., and J. Kadvany. 2011. *Risk: A very short introduction*. Oxford, United Kingdom: Oxford University Press.

Fischhoff, B., and D. Scheufele (Eds.). 2012. Arthur M. Sackler Colloquia: The science of science communication. *Proceedings of the National Academy of Sciences of the United States of America* online supplement. http://onlinedigeditions.com/publication/?i=174803 (accessed August 14, 2104). [Overviews and videos from both 2012 Science of Science Communication colloquia are available at http://www.nasonline.org/programs/sackler-colloquia/completed_colloquia/science-communication.html and http://www.nasonline.org/programs/sackler-colloquia/completed_colloquia/agenda-science-communication-II.html (accessed August 14, 2014).]

Fischhoff, B., S. Lichtenstein, P. Slovic, S. L. Derby, and R. L. Keeney. 1981. *Acceptable risk.* New York: Cambridge University Press.

Fischhoff, B., W. Bruine de Bruin, U. Güvenç, D. Caruso, and L. Brilliant. 2006. Analyzing disaster risks and plans: An avian flu example. *Journal of Risk and Uncertainty* 33:133-151.

Fischhoff, B., N. T. Brewer, and J. S. Downs, Eds. 2011. *Communicating risks and benefits: An evidence-based user's guide.* Washington, DC: U.S. Food and Drug Administration. http://www.fda.gov/AboutFDA/ReportsManualsForms/Reports/ucm268078.htm (accessed August 14, 2014).

Florig, H. K., M. G. Morgan, K. M. Morgan, K. E. Jenni, B. Fischhoff, P. S. Fischbeck, and M. DeKay. 2001. A deliberative method for ranking risks (2): Evaluation of validity and agreement among risk managers. *Risk Analysis* 21:923-938.

Funtowicz, S. O., and J. Ravetz. 1990. *Uncertainty and quality in science for policy.* Dordrecht, The Netherlands: Kluwer Academic Publishers.

Kahneman, D. 2011. *Thinking, fast and slow.* New York: Farrar Strauss & Giroux.

Krishnamurti, T., S. L. Eggers, and B. Fischhoff. 2008. The impact of over-the-counter availability of "Plan B" on teens' contraceptive decision-making. *Social Science & Medicine* 67:618-662.

Lichtenstein, S., and P. Slovic (Eds.). 2006. *The construction of preference.* New York: Cambridge University Press.

Morgan, M. G., and M. Henrion. 1990. *Uncertainty.* New York: Cambridge University Press.

NRC (National Research Council). 2011. Fischhoff, B., and C. Chauvin (Eds.). *Intelligence analysis: Behavioral and social science foundations.* Washington, DC: The National Academies Press. http://www.nap.edu/catalog.php?record_id=13062 (accessed August 14, 2014).

Schwartz, L. M., and S. Woloshin. 2013. The drug facts box: Improving the communication of prescription drug information. *Proceedings of the National Academy of Sciences of the United States of America* 110:14069-14074.

Slovic, P. (Ed.). 2000. *Perception of risk.* London, United Kingdom: Earthscan.

Workshop presentations by Lisa M. Schwartz and Steven Woloshin: Communicating Uncertainty About Benefits and Harms of Pharmaceutical Products

Downing, N. S., J. A. Aminawung, N. D. Shah, H. M. Krumholz, and J. S. Ross. 2014. Clinical trial evidence supporting FDA approval of novel therapeutic agents, 2005-2012. *Journal of the American Medical Association* 311(4):368-377.

Schwartz, L. M., and S. Woloshin. 2011. Communicating uncertainties about prescription drugs to the public: A national randomized trial. *JAMA Archives of Internal Medicine* 171(16):1463-1468.

Schwartz, L. M., S. Woloshin, A. Andrews, and T. A. Stukel. 2012. Influence of medical journal press releases on the quality of associated newspaper coverage: Retrospective cohort study. *British Medical Journal* 344:d8164.

Appendix D

Participant Biographies

Joseph Arvai, Ph.D., is Professor and Svare Chair in Applied Decision Research, Department of Geography, Institute for Sustainable Energy, Environment, and Economy, University of Calgary. His departmental homes are the Department of Geography, and the Institute for Sustainable Energy, Environment, and Economy. Dr. Arvai is also a Senior Researcher at Decision Research in Eugene, Oregon, and an Adjunct Professor in Engineering and Public Policy at Carnegie Mellon University. Dr. Arvai is an internationally recognized expert in the risk and decisions sciences; his research focuses on advancing our understanding of how people process information and make decisions, both as individuals and in groups. A second objective of his research is to develop and test decision support tools that can be used by people to improve decision quality across a wide range of environmental, social, and economic contexts; these include energy transitions, climate change, international development, space exploration, food security, health promotion, business and finance, and the protection of ecosystem services. Dr. Arvai's current research in these areas is supported by grants from the Canada School of Energy and Environment, the National Science Foundation, Carbon Management Canada, and the International Development Research Centre of Canada. In addition to Dr. Arvai's academic work, he is a member of the U.S. Environmental Protection Agency's Science Advisory Board, and a member of the U.S. National Academy of Sciences' (NAS's) Board on Environmental Change and Society. Dr. Arvai has also received several awards for his work. He was a recipient of the Chauncey Starr Award, which each year honors the individual age 40 or under who has made exceptional contributions to the field of risk and decision analysis. In 2011, he was named an Aldo Leopold Leadership Fellow by the Woods Institute for the Environment at Stanford University.

Kimby Barton, M.Sc., is Director, Bureau of Cardiology, Allergy and Neurological Sciences, Health Canada. Ms. Barton joined Health Canada in 2002 with the Marketed Pharmaceuticals and Medical Devices Bureau of the Marketed Health Products Directorate (MHPD). At MHPD, she was involved with development of methodologies for signal prioritization and signal assessment, and participated in a number of policy initiatives, including modernization of the Food and Drugs Act, as well as development of a Health Product Vigilance Framework. Ms. Barton has been the Director of the Bureau of Cardiology, Allergy and Neurological Sciences, in the Therapeutic Products Directorate, the group responsible for market authorization of drugs in these fields, since September 2009.

Carmen Bozic, M.D., is Senior Vice President, Clinical and Safety Sciences, Biogen Idec. Her department is responsible for managing clinical development, safety, and risk management, as well as preclinical safety for all products in the preapproval and postapproval phases within Biogen Idec's therapeutic focus areas of Neurology, Immunology, and Hematology. She has more than 15 years of industry experience overseeing clinical development programs, filings and launches in multiple therapeutic areas, and addressing complex issues in drug safety and benefit–risk management. Dr. Bozic led the development of the risk management plan for Tysabri (natalizumab) and presented on this topic at an FDA Advisory Committee. She has also served as a non-voting industry representative to the FDA's Risk Communication Advisory Committee. She received an M.D. and did her residency in Internal Medicine at McGill University in Montreal, Canada; completed a Fellowship in Pulmonary and Critical Care Medicine at Brigham and Women's Hospital in Boston; and was an Associate Physician at Beth Israel Deaconess Medical Center and Harvard Medical School before joining the biopharmaceutical industry. Dr. Bozic is a frequent lecturer and speaker on benefit–risk and other drug development topics nationally and internationally.

Baruch Fischhoff, Ph.D., M.A., is Howard Heinz University Professor, Department of Social and Decision Sciences, Department of Engineering and Public Policy, Carnegie Mellon University, where he heads the Decision Sciences major. A graduate of the Detroit Public Schools, he holds a B.S. in Mathematics and Psychology from Wayne State University and an M.A. and Ph.D. in Psychology from the Hebrew University of Jerusalem.

He is a member of the Institute of Medicine of The National Academies and is a past President of the Society for Judgment and Decision Making and of the Society for Risk Analysis. He chaired the FDA Risk Communication Advisory Committee and the National Research Council (NRC) Committee on Behavioral and Social Science Research to Improve Intelligence Analysis for National Security; he currently co-chairs the NRC Committee on Future Research Goals and Directions for Foundational Science in Cybersecurity. He was a member of the Eugene, Oregon, Commission on the Rights of Women, the Department of Homeland Security Science and Technology Advisory Committee, and the Environmental Protection Agency Scientific Advisory Board, where he chaired the Homeland Security Advisory Committee. He has written or edited several books: *Acceptable Risk* (1981), *A Two-State Solution in the Middle East: Prospects and Possibilities* (1993), *Preference Elicitation* (1999), *Risk Communication: The Mental Models Approach* (2001), *Communicating Risks and Benefits: An Evidence-Based User's Guide* (2011), *Intelligence Analysis: Behavioral and Social Science Foundations* (2011), *Judgment and Decision Making* (2011), *Risk: A Very Short Introduction* (2011), *Risk Analysis and Human Behavior* (2011), and *Counting Civilian Casualties* (2013).

Robert Fox, M.D., is Staff Neurologist, Mellen Center for Multiple Sclerosis and Vice-Chair for Research of the Neurological Institute, Cleveland Clinic. He received his M.D. from Johns Hopkins University, neurology training at the University of Pennsylvania, a master's degree in Clinical Research from Case Western Reserve University, and multiple sclerosis (MS) fellowship training at Cleveland Clinic. Dr. Fox's current research interests focus on clinical trials in MS, innovative magnetic resonance imaging, techniques to evaluate tissue recovery after injury and the effects of MS treatments, as well as MS patient decision making and tolerance to risk. He serves as an advisor for many clinical trials, including the Principal Investigator of the National Institutes of Health (NIH)-funded Phase II SPRINT-MS trial of ibudilast in progressive MS. In addition, he serves as the Managing Director of the NARCOMS MS Patient Registry, which currently follows more than 13,000 MS patients. Dr. Fox serves as a member of various advisory and review committees for the National MS Society and NIH, the General Advisory Council for the Cleveland Clinic Clinical Research Unit, and the Editorial Board of *Neurology and Multiple Sclerosis Journal*, and as a consultant to the pharmaceutical industry.

Patrick J. Frey, M.P.P., is the Director of the Office of Program and Strategic Analysis in the CDER at FDA. This office is deeply involved in numerous aspects of CDER's business, including the implementation and evaluation of significant CDER programs such as the PDUFA, Generic Drugs User

Fee Act (GDUFA), and Biosimilar User Fee Act of 2012 (BsUFA) programs, performance analysis and reporting of the user fee programs, economic analysis with respect to CDER's external stakeholder environment, lean management approaches to CDER's regulatory operations, and developing structured approaches to CDER's regulatory decision making. Before joining CDER, Mr. Frey was a Research Chemist at Merck & Co., Inc., in West Point, Pennsylvania, where he supported various drug development programs from the pre-Investigational New Drug phase through market launch. Mr. Frey received his B.S. in Chemistry from the University of Pittsburgh, and a master's in Public Policy from the Gerald R. Ford School of Public Policy at the University of Michigan.

Joel Greenhouse, Ph.D., M.P.H., is Professor of Statistics, Carnegie Mellon University, and Adjunct Professor of Psychiatry and Epidemiology at the University of Pittsburgh. He is a Fellow of the American Statistical Association and of the American Association for the Advancement of Science, and an elected Member of the International Statistical Institute. Professor Greenhouse has been a member of the NAS's Committee on National Statistics, the IOM's Committee on the Assessment of Family Violence Interventions, and the NRC panel on Statistical Issues for Research in the Combination of Information. He is an editor in chief for the journal *Statistics in Medicine*, and is a past editor of the Institute of Mathematical Statistics' Lecture Notes and Monograph Series. His research interests include applied Bayesian methods, methods for the analysis of data from longitudinal and observational studies, and methods for clinical trials. Professor Greenhouse is also interested in issues related to the use of research synthesis in practice, especially as it is used to synthesize evidence for scientific discovery and for making policy.

Tarek A. Hammad, M.D., Ph.D., M.Sc., M.S., FISPE, has recently joined Merck & Co., Inc., as an Executive Director in the Department of Epidemiology. Prior to joining Merck & Co., Inc. he was the Deputy Division Director of FDA's Division of Epidemiology located in the Office of Surveillance and Epidemiology (OSE) in CDER. In 2000, he joined the Divisions of Neurology and Psychiatry Drug Products in CDER as a drug safety Medical Reviewer and served as an active member of a multidisciplinary team that had overall responsibility for pre- and postmarketing safety evaluation of neurology and psychiatry drugs in the Divisions. Subsequently, in 2004, Dr. Hammad joined OSE as a Senior Medical Epidemiologist to work on large electronic medical records and insurance claims databases assessing postmarketing safety issues. He served as the Analytic Epidemiology Team Leader (2004) and as the Associate Director of Epidemiology (2008) in the same Division. Dr. Hammad has authored more than 60 peer-reviewed publications and made many presentations in various scientific conferences and other settings. He also holds several academic appointments, spanning various medical disciplines.

Ralph I. Horwitz, M.D., MACP, is Senior Vice President for Clinical Sciences Evaluation at GlaxoSmithKline, and Harold H. Hines, Jr. Professor Emeritus of Medicine and Epidemiology at Yale University. Dr. Horwitz trained in Internal Medicine at institutions (Royal Victoria Hospital of McGill University and the Massachusetts General Hospital) where science and clinical medicine were connected effortlessly. These experiences as a resident unleashed a deep interest in clinical research training, which he pursued as a Fellow in the Robert Wood Johnson Foundation Clinical Scholars Program at Yale under the direction of Alvan R. Feinstein. He joined the Yale faculty in 1978 and remained there for 25 years as Co-Director of the Clinical Scholars Program and later as Chair of the Department of Medicine. Dr. Horwitz's research has focused on the application of quantitative methods in design and analysis to the strategies of clinical care. Before joining GlaxoSmithKline, Dr. Horwitz was Chair of Medicine at Stanford University and Dean of Case Western Reserve Medical School. He is an elected member of the IOM, the American Society for Clinical Investigation, the American Epidemiological Society, and the Association of American Physicians (he was President in 2010). He was a member of the Advisory Committee to the NIH Director (under both Elias Zerhouni and Francis Collins). He currently serves on the scientific advisory board of IMEDS (Innovation in Medical Evidence Development and Surveillance) of the Reagan-Udall Foundation. Dr. Horwitz served on the American Board of Internal Medicine and was Chair in 2003. He is a Master of the American College of Physicians.

Alice Hughes, M.D., is the Deputy Director for Safety of the Division of Neurology at FDA's CDER. She oversees the identification, assessment, and management of postmarketing safety issues for drugs for neurological indications. Dr. Hughes joined FDA 11 years ago as a Medical Officer Safety Reviewer and subsequently was the leader of the division's safety group prior to assuming her current position. She has been extensively involved in the review of, and regulatory actions pertaining to, safety issues associated with (Tysabri) natalizumab, notably PML. She was the safety reviewer for Biogen's application for resumed marketing of Tysabri subject to a special restricted distribution program, which was approved in 2006. Dr. Hughes received a B.A. from Princeton University and an M.D. from the Mount Sinai School of Medicine prior to completing a residency in Internal Medicine at the Duke University Medical Center. She was a Morris Fishbein Fellow in Medical Editing at the *Journal of the*

American Medical Association before joining FDA. Dr. Hughes is Board Certified in Internal Medicine by the American Board of Internal Medicine.

Gavin Huntley-Fenner, Ph.D., is a Human Factors and Safety Consultant at Huntley-Fenner Advisors. He has a unique problem-solving skill set and communication style developed over more than 15 years as a researcher, author, educator, and business consultant. He regularly provides consumer product hazard analyses and has served as an expert witness for matters relating to risk perception, instruction manuals, warnings, labeling, safety and human development, human reaction time, and decision making. Dr. Huntley-Fenner is an educator and certified Continuing Legal Education provider, as well as a published author. Dr. Huntley-Fenner's consulting and forensic projects have involved a wide variety of types of products and situations, including consumer products, professional tools, medical devices, and human behavior in a variety of environments, including homes, schools, workplaces, and daytime and nighttime outdoor contexts. Dr. Huntley-Fenner's research employs a range of tools, including literature reviews, incident database analyses, statistics, experimental design, hazard and risk analyses, and specific human behavioral research methods such as surveys and human subjects testing. Recent research has focused on the impact of risk perception and design on product safety, an analysis of online consumer reviews for child safety–related content, a review of the effectiveness of auditory and visual warnings at railroad grade crossings, and a study on the impact of environmental signs on perceived risk. Dr. Huntley-Fenner's peer-reviewed and invited publications include "ANSI Z535.6 and Conspicuity: A Test of the New State of the Art Format for Instructional Manuals" (Proceedings of the Human Factors and Ergonomics Society) and "How will the Searchable Consumer Products Safety Incident Database Improve Product Safety" (Analysis and Perspective, Product Safety and Liability Reporter). Dr. Huntley-Fenner has been invited to speak at national and international scientific and non-scientific gatherings on topics ranging from basic and applied research to forensic consulting and to education. He is a member of the FDA Risk Communication Advisory Committee and he served as a member of California's Statewide Committee on Autism and Education. Prior to focusing full-time as a human factors consultant, Dr. Huntley-Fenner was a business consultant at McKinsey & Company. He began his professional career as an Assistant Professor at the University of California, Irvine (UCI). While on the UCI faculty, Dr. Huntley-Fenner's National Science Foundation (NSF)-supported research focused on problem solving, language processing and language development, cognitive development, and normal and abnormal brain development. Since 2005,

Dr. Huntley-Fenner has served as a Governing Board Member of the Irvine Unified School District.

John P. A. Ioannidis, M.D., D.Sc., holds the C. F. Rehnborg Professor in Disease Prevention, Stanford University, and is Professor of Health Research and Policy, and Director of the Stanford Prevention Research Center (SPRC), Stanford University School of Medicine, Professor of Statistics (by courtesy) at Stanford University School of Humanities and Sciences, and Director of the Meta-Research Innovation Center at Stanford (METRICS). From 1999 until 2010, he chaired the Department of Hygiene and Epidemiology at the School of Medicine, University of Ioannina in Greece, as a tenured professor since 2003. He graduated in the top rank of his class from the School of Medicine, University of Athens, in 1990 and also received a doctorate in Biopathology from the same institution. He trained at Harvard and Tufts, specializing in Internal Medicine and Infectious Diseases, and then held positions at NIH, Johns Hopkins University School of Medicine, and Tufts University School of Medicine. He has been Adjunct Professor of Medicine at Tufts, Adjunct Professor of Epidemiology at the Harvard School of Public Health, and Visiting Professor of Epidemiology and Biostatistics at Imperial College London. Dr. Ioannidis is a member of the executive board of the Human Genome Epidemiology Network, senior advisor on knowledge integration at the National Cancer Institute, and has served as President of the Society for Research Synthesis Methodology, and as a member of the editorial boards of 30 leading international journals. He has received several awards, including the European Award for Excellence in Clinical Science for 2007, and was inducted in the Association of American Physicians in 2009 and in the European Academy of Cancer Sciences in 2010.

John Jenkins, M.D., is currently the Director, Office of New Drugs, CDER, FDA. Dr. Jenkins received his undergraduate degree in Biology from East Tennessee State University in 1979 and his M.D. from the University of Tennessee at Memphis in 1983. He completed his postgraduate medical training in internal medicine, pulmonary disease, and critical care medicine at Virginia Commonwealth University/Medical College of Virginia from 1983 until 1988. Dr. Jenkins is Board Certified in Internal Medicine and Pulmonary Diseases by the American Board of Internal Medicine. Following completion of his medical training, Dr. Jenkins joined the faculty of Medical College of Virginia as an Assistant Professor of Pulmonary and Critical Care Medicine and as a Staff Physician at the Hunter Holmes McGuire Veterans Administration Medical Center in Richmond. Dr. Jenkins joined FDA as a Medical Officer in the Division of Oncology and Pulmonary Drug Products in 1992. He subsequently served as Pulmonary Medical Group Leader and Acting Division Director before being appointed as Director of the newly created Division of Pulmonary Drug Products in 1995. Dr. Jenkins became the Director of the Office of Drug Evaluation II in 1999 and served in that position until he was appointed to his current position in January 2002.

Michaela Kiernan, Ph.D., is a Senior Research Scientist at the SPRC at the Stanford University School of Medicine. She received her Ph.D. in Social/Health Psychology from Yale University. Funded by NIH and the American Heart Association (AHA), Dr. Kiernan's research focuses on testing behavioral interventions that promote long-term lifestyle changes and weight management among subgroups at risk, as well as developing methodological and statistical approaches that improve the design, delivery, and analysis of randomized clinical trials. The latter includes developing and testing recruitment and retention strategies for ethnic minorities and other underserved subgroups. Dr. Kiernan reviewed for the AHA Western States Affiliate Behavioral Science, Epidemiology, and Prevention Review Committee (2000–2003) and was a standing member of the NIH Psychosocial Risk and Disease Prevention Study Section (2009–2012). In 2002 and 2007, she was awarded the SPRC/Department of Medicine Divisional Teaching Award, and, in 2009, the Stanford University Postdoctoral Association Excellence in Mentoring Award.

Joyce Korvick, M.D., M.P.H., is currently the Deputy Director for Safety in the Division of Gastroenterology and Inborn Error Products, Office of Drug Evaluation III, CDER, FDA. In addition, she has extensive experience as a primary medical reviewer evaluating benefit–risk, having worked in several Divisions within CDER over the past 20 years. In her role as Deputy Director, she was intimately involved in the reintroduction of Lotronex to the market. Over the past several years, she has been involved in numerous benefit–risk assessments for gastroenterological therapies. Dr. Korvick is trained in Internal Medicine, as well as Infectious Diseases. She is a Fellow of the Infectious Diseases Society of America. Previously she worked for the NIH in the Division of AIDS developing the clinical trials for AIDS: ACTG and CPCRA. During that period, she served as a member of the NIH institutional review board. Her academic experience includes Assistant Professor of Medicine at the University of Kentucky, Lexington, where she was the Chair of the Infection Control Board. She has published numerous papers, and has served as a peer reviewer for several medical journals. Dr. Korvick's extensive clinical trials and regulatory experience gives her a unique perspective on benefit–risk and drug development.

Lisa LaVange, Ph.D., is Director of the Office of Biostatistics in the Office of Translational Sciences, CDER, FDA. She assumed this position in September 2011, and as Director, oversees approximately 170 statistical reviewers and staff members involved in the development and application of statistical methodology for drug regulation. Prior to joining FDA, Dr. LaVange was Professor and Director of the Collaborative Studies Coordinating Center in the Department of Biostatistics, Gillings School of Global Public Health at the University of North Carolina at Chapel Hill. As Center Director, she served as Principal Investigator of the coordinating centers for several large-scale multicenter studies. Before joining academia, Dr. LaVange spent 10 years in the pharmaceutical industry, serving as vice president for a small pharmaceutical company and for a large, global contract research organization. Dr. LaVange is a Fellow of the American Statistical Association and served as President of the Eastern North American Region of the International Biometric Society (2007). She is co-editor of the *Journal of Pharmaceutical Statistics* and editor in chief of the ASA-SIAM book series. Her research areas include methods for the design and analysis of clinical trials and complex sample survey data. She taught graduate courses at University of North Carolina in the areas of clinical trials, statistical consulting, and statistical leadership.

Robyn Lim, Ph.D., is Senior Science Advisor with the Office of Legislative and Regulatory Modernization, Health Products and Food Branch, Health Canada, bringing technical and review-related perspectives to the development of Canada's modernized drug regulatory system since the project's inception in late 2005. In this capacity, Dr. Lim developed the benefit–risk–based evidence standard and concepts for market authorization and benefit–harm–uncertainty management for the new Canadian drug regulatory framework and has presented these and related issues at a variety of international meetings since 2007. Prior to joining the modernization team, Dr. Lim was a Health Canada clinical and non-clinical safety and effectiveness reviewer (with the Therapeutic Products Directorate, since 1996) and assessed drug submissions across product lifecycle (clinical trial applications, pre- and postmarket drug submissions) and other drug issues, primarily in the fields of analgesia, anesthesia, neurology, and psychiatry. Dr. Lim has participated on Health Canada intra- and inter-Directorate working groups, such as Good Review Practices (and developed TPD's Good Review Guiding Principles) and Adaptive Trial Design and at Departmental Expert Advisory Committee meetings. She was also nominated and served on the U.S. Pharmacopeia Neurology Expert Committee (2000–2005). Since 2007, Dr. Lim has participated in a number of international public–private endeavors focused on benefit–risk–uncertainty science. Dr. Lim has received Health Canada Awards for Excellence in Risk Management (2001) and for Creativity and Innovation (2007) for her review work and as part of the modernization team, respectively. In 2012, Dr. Lim also received an honor from the editors of the *Journal of Pharmacoepidemiology and Drug Safety* for best peer reviewer performance. Dr. Lim received bachelor's and master's degrees from the Biochemistry Department, Queen's University at Kingston, Ontario, Canada, and a doctorate in Molecular Neurophysiology from the Physiological Laboratory, University of Cambridge, United Kingdom, and Trinity College, Cambridge, United Kingdom.

David R. Mandel, M.Sc., Ph.D., is Senior Scientist, Socio-Cognitive Systems, Defence Research and Development Canada (DRDC), Toronto Research Centre. He earned a B.A. in Psychology from Concordia University and M.A. and Ph.D. in Psychology from University of British Columbia. He was a Social Sciences and Humanities Research Council Postdoctoral Fellow at Stanford University. He held academic positions as a Senior Lecturer at University of Herfordshire and, later, as a tenured Associate Professor at University of Victoria. He is currently a senior defence scientist in the Sensemaking and Decision Group of the Socio-Cognitive Systems Section at DRDC's Toronto Research Centre. He is also Adjunct Professor of Psychology at York University. His research examines the coherence and accuracy of human judgment and decision making under conditions of uncertainty. He has served as a scientific advisor to such organizations as the NAS, NIH, Office of the Director of National Intelligence, U.S. Department of Defense, and NATO. His books include *The Psychology of Counterfactual Thinking* and *Neuroscience of Decision Making.*

Charles F. Manski, Ph.D., has been Board of Trustees Professor in Economics at Northwestern University since 1997. He previously was a faculty member at the University of Wisconsin–Madison, the Hebrew University of Jerusalem, and Carnegie Mellon University. He received his B.S. and Ph.D. in Economics from Massachusetts Institute of Technology in 1970 and 1973. Dr. Manski's research spans econometrics, judgement and decision, and the analysis of social policy. He is author of *Public Policy in an Uncertain World* (Harvard, 2013), *Identification for Prediction and Decision* (Harvard, 2007), *Social Choice with Partial Knowledge of Treatment Response* (Princeton, 2005), *Partial Identification of Probability Distributions* (Springer, 2003), *Identification Problems in the Social Sciences* (Harvard, 1995), and *Analog Estimation Methods in Econometrics* (Chapman & Hall, 1988); co-author of *College Choice in America* (Harvard, 1983); and co-editor of *Evaluating Welfare and Training Programs* (Harvard, 1992) and *Structural Analysis of Discrete Data with Econometric Applications* (MIT, 1981). He has served as

Director of the Institute for Research on Poverty and as Chair of the Board of Overseers of the Panel Study of Income Dynamics. Editorial service includes terms as editor of the *Journal of Human Resources*, co-editor of the *Econometric Society Monograph Series*, member of the Editorial Board of the *Annual Review of Economics*, and associate editor of the *Annals of Applied Statistics*, *Econometrica*, *Journal of Economic Perspectives*, *Journal of the American Statistical Association*, and *Transportation Science*. Service at the NRC includes being Chair of the Committee on Data and Research for Policy on Illegal Drugs and a member of the Report Review Committee, the Committee on Law and Justice, the Board on Mathematical Sciences and their Applications, the Committee on National Statistics, and the Commission on Behavioral and Social Sciences and Education. Dr. Manski is an elected member of the NAS, and an elected Fellow of the Econometric Society, the American Academy of Arts and Sciences, and the American Association for the Advancement of Science.

Kimberly McCleary is Director of Strategic Initiatives at *FasterCures*, a center of the Milken Institute determined to remove barriers to medical progress. At *FasterCures*, Ms. McCleary leads the charge on key programmatic areas, including FDA and how it evaluates risk and benefit for patients, and medical innovation and how we determine value and reimbursement. Prior to joining *FasterCures*' staff, she was President and CEO of the CFIDS Association of America from 1991 to 2013. She earned a reputation as an articulate patient advocate, a keen policy strategist, a diplomatic bridge builder, and a dedicated servant leader. She has worked with leaders throughout the executive and legislative branches to develop, implement, and oversee effective policy. Ms. McCleary helped found the Chronic Pain Research Alliance and joined with other leaders and Pfizer to establish the Campaign to End Women's Pain in 2010. She led the Partnering to End Pain project selected by Sanofi U.S. as a finalist in the 2012 Collaborate/Activate Innovation Challenge. She has participated in every opportunity organized by FDA to shape its Patient-Focused Drug Development Initiative (PFDDI), including a range of consultations leading up the first of the 20 PFDDI workshops focused on chronic fatigue syndrome and myalgic encephalopathy held in April 2013. With leaders in the narcolepsy community, Ms. McCleary helped design and launch the Unite Narcolepsy initiative to educate, engage, and empower narcolepsy patients and their advocates to participate effectively in the PFDDI meeting held in September 2013. She is a graduate of the University of North Carolina at Chapel Hill.

Timothy McDaniels, Ph.D., M.A., is Professor, Faculty of Science, Institute of Resources and Environment, University of British Columbia. Dr.

McDaniels received his Ph.D. from Carnegie Mellon University. He is a specialist in decision sciences and policy analysis, particularly in managing environmental and technology-related societal risks. His current research focuses on climate change adaptation in linked human/ecological systems. Dr. McDaniels is a professor appointed in two graduate interdisciplinary programs at the University of British Columbia. He served as the Director of the Institute for Resources, Environment and Sustainability, and also as the interim Principal of the College for Interdisciplinary Studies. He also has served on expert panels for the NAS, NOAA, the Environmental Protection Agency, Health Canada, and other organizations. He has participated in advisory roles for several Canadian inquiries and panels regarding risk issues. He was a co-investigator in the Climate and Energy Decision Making Center at Carnegie Mellon University in Pittsburgh. In 2008, he was appointed to the NAS Committee on the Human Dimensions of Global Change. He served as the Decision Sciences area editor of the journal *Risk Analysis* for 8 years, and is a Fellow of the Society for Risk Analysis.

M. Granger Morgan, Ph.D., M.S., is Professor and Head of the Department of Engineering and Public Policy, Carnegie Mellon University, where he is also University and Lord Chair Professor in Engineering. In addition, he holds academic appointments in the Department of Electrical and Computer Engineering and in the H. John Heinz III College. His research addresses problems in science, technology, and public policy, with a particular focus on energy, environmental systems, climate change, and risk analysis. Much of his work has involved the development and demonstration of methods to characterize and treat uncertainty in quantitative policy analysis. At Carnegie Mellon, Dr. Morgan directs the NSF Center for Climate and Energy Decision Making (www.cedmcenter.org). He is also Director of the campus-wide Wilton E. Scott Institute for Energy Innovation (www.cmu.edu/energy). Dr. Morgan serves as Chair of the Scientific and Technical Council for the International Risk Governance Council. He is a Member of the NAS, and a Fellow of the American Association for the Advancement of Science, the Institute of Electrical and Electronics Engineers, and the Society for Risk Analysis. He holds a B.A. from Harvard College, where he concentrated in Physics, an M.S. in Astronomy and Space Science from Cornell University, and a Ph.D. from the Department of Applied Physics and Information Sciences at the University of California, San Diego.

Theresa Mullin, Ph.D., is Director, Office of Strategic Programs, CDER, FDA. As Director of the CDER Office of Strategic Programs, Dr. Mullin leads CDER strategic planning and directs the CDER international program, business informatics, drug data standards, and program and strategic analysis. This includes leading FDA development of a drug benefit–risk assessment framework, and Patient-Focused Drug Development initiative. In addition, Dr. Mullin heads the FDA delegation to International Conference on Harmonization (ICH), leading the U.S. discussion of the future of ICH. She served as the FDA lead negotiator for the 2012 reauthorization of the PDUFA providing an estimated $700 million in annual fee revenues. She also served as lead negotiator for new user fees for biosimilar biological products authorized under the Biologics Price Competition and Innovation Act of 2009. Prior to joining CDER in 2007, Dr. Mullin was Assistant Commissioner for Planning in the FDA Office of Commissioner, where she led FDA user fee negotiations with the pharmaceutical industry for both the 2007 and the 2002 reauthorizations of PDUFA. Since joining FDA, Dr. Mullin has received a number of awards, including the Senior Executive Service Presidential Rank Award for Distinguished Service in 2011 and Presidential Rank Award for Meritorious Service in 2006, as well as the FDA Commissioner's Award of Excellence. Prior to work at FDA, Dr. Mullin was a Senior Manager with The Lewin Group, specializing in health care consulting, and Principal Scientist at Decision Science Consortium, specializing in decision research and analysis. Dr. Mullin received her B.A. magna cum laude in Economics from Boston College and Ph.D. in Public Policy Analysis from Carnegie Mellon University.

Mary H. Parks, M.D., is currently the Deputy Director in the Office of Drug Evaluation II, Office of New Drugs, CDER, FDA, which oversees therapies developed in the Division of Metabolism and Endocrinology Products, Division of Anesthesia, Analgesia, and Addiction Products, and Division of Pulmonary, Allergy, and Rheumatology Products. Dr. Parks is a board-certified endocrinologist and internist and received her medical training and degree from Tufts University Medical School and Georgetown University School and Medical Center. She joined FDA as a Medical Officer in 1998 in the Division of Metabolism and Endocrinology Products, where she served as Division Director from 2006 through 2013.

Francesco Pignatti, M.D., is Head of Oncology, Hematology, Diagnostics Section, Scientific and Regulatory Management Department, Human Medicines Evaluation Division, EMA. Dr. Pignatti earned his M.D. at the University of Rome La Sapienza. In 1995 he became Research Fellow at the EORTC Data Center, Brussels, Belgium, where he was involved in numerous activities, including clinical trial design, conduct, analysis, and reporting. In 1997 he became Medical Advisor for the Gastrointestinal

Tract Cancer Cooperative Group and Brain Tumor Cooperative Group. In 1997 he obtained an M.S. in Biostatistics from the University of Limbourg, Belgium. In 1999 he joined the EMA in London. Since 2009, he has held the position of Head of Oncology, Haematology, and Diagnostics in the Human Medicines Evaluation Division.

Jennifer R. Pippins, M.D., M.P.H., is a Medical Officer in the Division of Pulmonary, Allergy, and Rheumatology Products, Office of New Drugs, CDER, FDA. Dr. Pippins attended Harvard College and Harvard Medical School, and completed a combined internal medicine–pediatrics internship and residency at the Harvard Combined Med/Peds Program. After completing residency, she was a General Internal Medicine Research Fellow at Brigham and Women's Hospital, where she focused on health disparities. She left Boston and relocated in the Washington, DC, area, first as an AcademyHealth Health Policy Fellow at the National Center for Health Statistics, and subsequently as a Medical Officer with FDA, in what is now the Division of Pulmonary, Allergy, and Rheumatology Drugs within FDA's CDER/Office of New Drugs.

Robert E. Ratner, M.D., FACP, FACE, is Chief Scientific and Medical Officer for the American Diabetes Association, where he provides leadership and oversight of scientific and medical activities, including research, clinical affairs, program recognition and certification, medical information, and professional education. In this capacity, he oversees the Association's support of a broad range of professional education activities and the development of the Association's Clinical Practice Recommendations, clinical consensus reports, and expert opinions. Prior to joining the American Diabetes Association, Dr. Ratner was a Professor of Medicine at Georgetown University Medical School and Senior Research Scientist at the MedStar Health Research Institute in Washington, DC. In 2012 he completed a sabbatical as a Robert Wood Johnson Foundation Health Policy Fellow, having served as the study director for the IOM Comparative Effectiveness Research Priorities Committee, and as a program examiner for health reform in the Health Division of the U.S. Office of Management and Budget. He received his M.D. from Baylor College of Medicine, where he also completed his Internal Medicine training. He underwent Fellowship training in Endocrinology and Metabolism at Harvard Medical School and the Joslin Diabetes Center in Boston. Dr. Ratner recently completed 6 years of service on the Steering Committee of the National Diabetes Education Program, representing the American Diabetes Association. He has served on the Board of Directors of the National Certification Board for Diabetes Education and the American Association of Diabetes Educators, and is past President of the Washington Area Affiliate of the American Diabetes Association. His research interests include diabetes therapeutics and complications, with an emphasis on translational efforts from controlled trials into community-based practice. He is the author of more than 120 original scientific articles and 20 book chapters.

Sebastian Schneeweiss, M.D., Sc.D., is Professor of Medicine and Epidemiology at Harvard Medical School and Vice Chief of the Division of Pharmacoepidemiology and Pharmacoeconomics of the Department of Medicine, Brigham and Women's Hospital. He is Principal Investigator (PI) of the Harvard-Brigham Drug Safety Research Center funded by FDA/CDER, and Methods Lead of the FDA Mini-Sentinel program. His research is funded by multiple grants from NIH, Patient-Centered Outcomes Research Institute, Agency for Healthcare Research and Quality, and FDA and focuses on the comparative effectiveness and safety of biopharmaceuticals and analytic methods to improve the validity of epidemiologic studies using complex health care databases, particularly for newly marketed medical products. His work is published in high-ranking journals. Dr. Schneeweiss is past President of the International Society for Pharmacoepidemiology and is Fellow of the American College of Epidemiology, the American College of Clinical Pharmacology, and the International Society for Pharmacoepidemiology. He is voting consultant to the FDA Drug Safety and Risk Management Advisory Committee and member of the Methods Committee of the Patient-Centered Outcomes Research Institute. He received his medical training at the University of Munich Medical School and his doctoral degree in Pharmacoepidemiology from Harvard University.

Lisa M. Schwartz, M.D., M.S., is Professor, Departments of Medicine and Community & Family Medicine, Dartmouth Medical School, and Co-Director, Center for Medicine and the Media, at The Dartmouth Institute for Health Policy and Clinical Practice. Dr. Schwartz graduated from New York University School of Medicine and completed internal medicine residency at the New York University/Bellevue Hospital program in New York City. She received an M.S. at the Center for the Evaluative Clinical Sciences at Dartmouth. She is the Co-Director of the Center for Medicine and the Media at The Dartmouth Institute for Health Policy and Clinical Practice, and former co-Director of the VA Outcomes Group (White River Junction, Vermont). Together with Dr. Steven Woloshin, she has worked to improve communication of medical evidence to physicians, journalists, and the public (specifically focusing on screening, prescription drugs, and statistics). She is a co-author of two books: *Know Your Chances* and *Overdi-*

agnosed; she is an occasional columnist for the *British Medical Journal*, and her essays have appeared in *The New York Times* and *The Washington Post*.

Paul J. Seligman, M.D., M.P.H., is currently Executive Director for U.S. Regulatory Policy at Amgen Inc. Prior to joining Amgen in 2012, he had a public health career of nearly 30 years in the federal government. At FDA he served as the Director of FDA's Latin America Regional Office, as Associate Director for Safety Policy and Communication in CDER, and as the Director of the Office of Pharmacoepidemiology and Statistical Science. Before joining FDA in July 2001, Dr. Seligman served for 7 years as the Deputy Assistant Secretary for Health Studies at the U.S. Department of Energy. He began his Public Health Service (PHS) career in 1983 at the Centers for Disease Control and Prevention (CDC) as an Epidemic Intelligence Service Officer. He completed a primary care internal medicine residency at The Cambridge Hospital in Cambridge, Massachusetts, prior to joining CDC. From 1974 to 1976, he was a Peace Corps volunteer in Kenya. Dr. Seligman holds an M.D. from the University of California, Davis, an M.P.H. in Industrial Health from the University of Michigan, and a B.S. in Chemistry from Yale University. He is Board Certified in Internal Medicine, Occupational Medicine, and Public Health, and General Preventive Medicine. He is a retired Commissioned Officer from PHS, having attained the rank of Rear Admiral.

Cynthia Sitcov is a Patient Representative & Voting Member of the FDA Central and Peripheral Systems Advisory Committee. Ms. Sitcov attended the State University of New York at Buffalo. She is an executive recruiter specializing in attorney recruitment. She was diagnosed with MS in 1975. For the past 5 years, she has served as a patient representative on FDA's Peripheral and Central Nervous System Advisory Committee as a voting member. The committees she has participated in include the review of the following MS drugs: Tysabri, Gilenya, Ampyra, and most recently Lemtrada. She has appeared on panels for the National MS Society, NAS, and FDA.

Brian L. Strom, M.D., M.P.H., is the recently appointed Inaugural Chancellor of Rutgers Biomedical and Health Sciences (RBHS) and the Executive Vice President for Health Affairs at Rutgers University. RBHS has nine schools and five centers/institutes, and includes academic, patient care, and research facilities. These are most of the units of the former University of Medicine and Dentistry of New Jersey (UMDNJ), now dissolved, several Rutgers University units with health-related missions, and two research units historically co-managed by Rutgers and UMDNJ. The integration of these entities is designed to create a single organization that will lead to new models for clinical care and community service, educate the next generation of health care providers using health care team approaches, and conduct research. Dr. Strom was formerly the Executive Vice Dean of Institutional Affairs, Founding Chair of the Department of Biostatistics and Epidemiology, Founding Director of the Center for Clinical Epidemiology and Biostatistics, and Founding Director of the Graduate Program in Epidemiology and Biostatistics, all at the Perelman School of Medicine of the University of Pennsylvania (Penn). Dr. Strom earned a B.S. in Molecular Biophysics and Biochemistry from Yale University and an M.D. from the Johns Hopkins University School of Medicine in 1975. He was an intern and resident in Internal Medicine and an NIH Fellow in Clinical Pharmacology at the University of California, San Francisco. He simultaneously earned an M.P.H. in Epidemiology at the University of California, Berkeley. He has been on the faculty of the Penn School of Medicine since 1980. The Center for Clinical Epidemiology and Biostatistics (CCEB) that he created at Penn includes more than 550 faculty, research and support staff, and trainees. At the time Dr. Strom stepped down, CCEB research received nearly $49 million/year in extramural support. Its total budget was approximately $67 million. Although Dr. Strom's interests span many areas of clinical epidemiology, his major research interest is in the field of pharmacoepidemiology, that is, the application of epidemiologic methods to the study of drug use and effects. He is recognized as a founder of this field and for his pioneer work in using large automated databases for research. He is editor of the field's major text (now in its fifth edition) and editor in chief for *Pharmacoepidemiology and Drug Safety*, the official journal of the International Society for Pharmacoepidemiology. As one of many specific contributions, his research was pivotal in prompting the American Heart Association and American Dental Association to reverse 50 years of guidelines, and recommend against use of antibiotics to prevent infective endocarditis, instead of recommending for this widespread practice. In addition to writing more than 580 papers, and 14 books, he has been PI for more than 275 grants, including more than $115 million in direct costs alone. Dr. Strom has been invited to give more than 400 talks outside his local area, including presentations as the keynote speaker for numerous international meetings. He has been a consultant to NIH, FDA, CDC, U.S. Pharmacopeia, Association of American Medical Colleges, Joint Commission on the Accreditation of Healthcare Organizations, foreign governments, most major pharmaceutical manufacturers, and many law firms. Dr. Strom is also a nationally recognized leader in clinical research training. At the Perelman School of Medicine, Dr. Strom developed graduate training programs in epidemiology and biostatistics. More than 625 clinicians have been trained or are in training through the largest of these training programs, which leads to a Master of

Science in Clinical Epidemiology degree. All but approximately 65 former trainees in this program have appointments in academic or other research institutions. Dr. Strom was PI or Co-PI of 11 different NIH-funded clinical epidemiology trainees. The NIH training grants (T32, D43, K12, and K30) supported the clinical epidemiology trainees in many different specialties and subspecialties. Dr. Strom has also been the primary mentor for more than 40 clinical research trainees, former and current, and numerous junior faculty members. Internationally, Dr. Strom was a key contributor to the conceptualization and planning that led to the development of the International Clinical Epidemiology Network (INCLEN), created in 1979 with support provided by the Rockefeller Foundation to provide clinical research training to clinicians from selected developing country sites. Penn was an INCLEN founding member and one of five training centers. INCLEN Phase I, from 1979 through 1995, resulted in the establishment of 26 clinical epidemiology units in Africa, India, Latin America, and Southeast Asia. The Penn training program alone, led by Dr. Strom, trained 63 INCLEN trainees. Dr. Strom was a member of the Board of Regents of the American College of Physicians, the Board of Directors of the American Society for Clinical Pharmacology and Therapeutics, and the Board of Directors for the American College of Epidemiology, and is currently a member of the Board of Directors for the Association for Patient-Oriented Research. He was previously President of the International Society for Pharmacoepidemiology and the Association for Clinical Research Training. Dr. Strom was on the Drug Utilization Review Committee and the Gerontology Committee of the U.S. Pharmacopoeia, served on the Drug Safety and Risk Management Advisory Committee for FDA, chaired the IOM Committee to Assess the Safety and Efficacy of the Anthrax Vaccine, chaired the IOM Committee on Smallpox Vaccine Program Implementation, chaired the IOM Committee to Review NIOSH's Traumatic Injury Program, chaired the IOM Committee on the Consequences of Reducing Sodium in the Population, was a member of the IOM Committee to Review the CDC Anthrax Vaccine Safety and Efficacy Research Program, and was a member of the IOM Committee on Standards for Developing Trustworthy Clinical Practice Guidelines. Dr. Strom is a member of the American Epidemiology Society, and is one of a handful of clinical epidemiologists ever elected to the American Society of Clinical Investigation and American Association of Physicians. He has also been an elected member of the IOM of the NAS since 2001. Dr. Strom received the 2003 Rawls-Palmer Progress in Medicine Award from the American Society for Clinical Pharmacology and Therapeutics, the Naomi M. Kanof Clinical Investigator Award of the Society for Investigative Dermatology, the George S. Pepper Professorship of Public Health and Preventive Medicine, and in 2006 he received the Sustained Scientific Excellence Award from the International Society for Pharmacoepidemiology. In addition, Dr. Strom was named the 2008 recipient of the John Phillips Memorial Award for Outstanding Work in Clinical Medicine. This award is from the American College of Physicians (ACP) and is considered to be one of the highest awards in Internal Medicine. Dr. Strom also received the 2013 Association for Clinical and Translational Science/American Federation for Medical Research National Award for Career Achievement and Contribution to Clinical and Translational Science for translation from clinical use into public benefit and policy. Penn awards that Dr. Strom received include the Class of 1992 Class Teaching Award and the Samuel Martin Health Evaluation Sciences Research Award. Dr. Strom received the 2004 Christian R. and Mary F. Lindback Award, the university's most prestigious teaching award, in recognition of the contribution he has made in his career to clinical research teaching.

Robert Temple, M.D., is Deputy Director for Clinical Science and Acting Deputy Director, Office of Drug Evaluation I, CDRE, FDA. Dr. Temple received his M.D. from the New York University School of Medicine. In 1972, he joined CDER as a review Medical Officer in the Division of Metabolic and Endocrine Drug Products. He later moved into the position of Director of the Division of Cardio-Renal Drug Products. In his current position, Dr. Temple oversees ODE-1, which is responsible for the regulation of cardio-renal, neuropharmacologic, and psychopharmacologic drug products. Dr. Temple has a longstanding interest in the design and conduct of clinical trials and has written extensively on this subject, especially on choice of control group in clinical trials, evaluation of active control trials, trials to evaluate dose–response, and trials using "enrichment" designs. He also has a longstanding interest in hepatotoxicity of drugs, having participated in the first detailed FDA–NIH-outside discussion of the subject in 1978.

Steven Woloshin, M.D., M.S., is Professor, Departments of Medicine and Community & Family Medicine, Dartmouth Medical School, and Co-Director, Center for Medicine and the Media, at The Dartmouth Institute for Health Policy and Clinical Practice. Dr. Woloshin graduated from Boston University School of Medicine and completed an internal medicine residency at the New York University/Bellevue Hospital program in New York City. He received an M.S. at the Center for the Evaluative Clinical Sciences at Dartmouth. He is the Co-Director of the Center for Medicine and the Media at The Dartmouth Institute for Health Policy and Clinical Practice, and former Co-Director of the VA Outcomes Group (White River Junction, Vermont). Together with Dr. Lisa M. Schwartz, he has worked to improve communication of medical evidence to physicians, journalists, and the public (specifically focusing on screening, prescription drugs, and statistics). He is a co-author of two books: *Know Your Chances* and *Overdiagnosed;* he is an occasional columnist for the *British Medical Journal*, and his essays have appeared in *The New York Times* and *The Washington Post*.

Janet Woodcock, M.D., is Director, CDER, FDA. Dr. Woodcock joined FDA in 1986, assuming the leadership of CDER in May 1994. Prior to joining CDER, she served as Acting Deputy Center Director of the Center for Biologics Evaluation and Research (1990–1992) and Director of the Office of Therapeutics Research and Review (1992–1994), where she oversaw approval of the first biotechnology-based treatments for MS and cystic fibrosis. From 2004 to 2008, Dr. Woodcock provided support to FDA's Commissioner, serving as Deputy Commissioner for Operations and Chief Medical Officer. During her tenure at FDA, Dr. Woodcock's achievements have been substantial. Under her leadership, CDER has streamlined review processes for new and generic drugs while improving standards for quality, safety, and effectiveness. The submission of marketing applications and adverse events reports and the review of submissions in FDA have been transitioned to electronic formats. CDER's regulatory decision-making processes have also been streamlined, making decisions more open and transparent. CDER's regulatory procedures and policies are publicly available—scores of technical guidances describing FDA's thinking on regulatory standards have been issued. Many CDER processes are carried out with an unprecedented degree of participation on the part of consumer and patient representatives. An extensive CDER website hosts a myriad of helpful information on drug approvals, safety issues, and other critical information targeting consumers, patients, health care practitioners, regulated industry, and other audiences. Highlights of selected recent accomplishments include negotiations of the 2012 GDUFA, which will speed access to safe and effective generic drugs to the public and reduce costs to industry, and the PDUFA V to support timely evaluation and approval of new drugs. PDUFA V has a particular emphasis on patient-focused drug development. In 2011 and 2012, Dr. Woodcock launched multiple efforts to support development of new therapies for rare and neglected diseases and new antibacterial therapies. She oversaw the implementation of innovative policies to foster adaptive trial designs (2010) and trial enrichment strategies (2012) and encouraged the qualification of new drug development tools (2010) to help speed drug development and evaluation. Following enactment in March 2010 of the Patient Protection and Affordable Care Act (Affordable Care Act), Dr. Woodcock developed and launched the biosimilars effort to create an abbreviated licensure pathway for biological products, then worked on negotiating the BsUFA to support approval using this new pathway.

Dr. Woodcock continues to lead FDA's Pharmaceutical Quality for the 21st Century initiative, to modernize pharmaceutical manufacturing, and the Safe Use/Safety First initiatives, which are critical to managing drug safety throughout the drug lifecycle and ensuring frequent and clear communications to the public about the risks and benefits of drugs. As Acting Deputy Commissioner for Operations, in 2004, Dr. Woodcock led the Critical Path Initiative, which continues to encourage and foster the development of new and better tools to support medical product research so that drug, device, and biologics development is more predictable and more informative. As Deputy Commissioner and Chief Medical Officer, Dr. Woodcock launched the Sentinel Initiative with the goal of building a new active surveillance system to augment FDA's existing adverse events monitoring systems. The resulting Mini-Sentinel pilot program, now used to assess safety signals, can access data on more than 130,000 people. As Director of CDER, Dr. Woodcock maintains contact with a variety of diverse constituencies, including the clinical and scientific communities, members of Congress and the administration, the national media, patient and consumer advocacy groups, the international drug regulatory community, regulated industry, and representatives of federal and state agencies. She frequently appears in or is quoted by the national media and has testified repeatedly before Congress. Dr. Woodcock has earned numerous awards, most recently, the Arthritis Foundation's Floyd B. Odlum Making a Difference Award and the Luminary Award from the Personalized Medicine World Conference. She has been the recipient of the Presidential Rank Meritorious Executive Award and three Health and Human Services Secretary's Distinguished Service Awards, among many others. She has authored more than 60 publications. Dr. Woodcock received her M.D. from Northwestern University Medical School, following an undergraduate degree in Chemistry from Bucknell University.

Deborah A. Zarin, M.D., is Director, ClinicalTrials.gov, National Library of Medicine, NIH. In this capacity, Dr. Zarin oversees the development and operation of an international registry and results reporting system for clinical trials, and the corresponding implementation of legal and other trial reporting policies. Dr. Zarin's recent research has been on the quality of trial reporting, as well as issues in the design and analysis of clinical trials. Previous positions held by Dr. Zarin include the Director, Technology Assessment Program, at the Agency for Healthcare Research and Quality, and the Director of the Practice Guidelines program at the American Psychiatric Association. In these positions, Dr. Zarin conducted systematic reviews and related analyses in support of evidence-based clinical and policy recommendations. Dr. Zarin's academic interests are in the area of evidence-based clinical and policy decision making, as well as clinical trial conduct, analysis, and reporting. She is the author of more than 70 peer-reviewed articles. Dr. Zarin graduated from Stanford University and received her doctorate in medicine from Harvard Medical School. She completed a clinical decision-making fellowship, a pediatric internship, and is Board Certified in General Psychiatry, as well as in Child and Adolescent Psychiatry.